Virtue as Social Inte

Virtue as Social Intelligence: An Empirically Grounded Theory takes on the claims of philosophical situationism, the ethical theory that is skeptical about the possibility of human virtue. Influenced by social psychological studies, philosophical situationists argue that human personality is too fluid and fragmented to support a stable set of virtues. They claim that virtue cannot be grounded in empirical psychology. This book argues otherwise.

Drawing on the work of psychologists Walter Mischel and Yuichi Shoda, Nancy E. Snow argues that the social psychological experiments that philosophical situationists rely on look at the wrong kinds of situations to test for behavioral consistency. Rather than looking at situations that are objectively similar, researchers need to compare situations that have similar meanings *for the subject*. When this is done, subjects exhibit behavioural consistencies that warrant the attribution of enduring traits and virtues are a subset of these traits. Virtue can thus be empirically grounded, and virtue ethics has nothing to fear from philosophical situationism.

Nancy E. Snow is an Associate Professor of Philosophy at Marquette University in Milwaukee, Wisconsin. She has published on empathy, compassion, humility, and other topics relevant to moral psychology and virtue ethics.

Virtue as Social Intelligence

An Empirically Grounded Theory

Nancy E. Snow

Routledge
Taylor & Francis Group
NEW YORK AND LONDON

First published 2010
by Routledge
711 ThirdAve, New York, NY 10017

Simultaneously published in the UK
by Routledge
2 Park Square, Milton Park, Abingdon, Oxon OX14 4RN

Routledge is an imprint of the Taylor & Francis Group, an informa business

Typeset in Minion by EvS Communication Networx, Inc.

Library of Congress Cataloging in Publication Data
Snow, Nancy E.
Virtue as social intelligence : an empirically grounded theory / Nancy E. Snow.
p. cm.
1. Ethics. 2. Virtue. I. Title.
BJ1521.S66 2009
179'.9—dc22
2009013195

ISBN 10: 0-415-99909-X (hbk)
ISBN 10: 0-415-99910-3 (pbk)
ISBN 10: 0-203-88057-9 (ebk)

ISBN 13: 978-0-415-99909-0 (hbk)
ISBN 13: 978-0-415-99910-6 (pbk)
ISBN 13: 978-0-203-88057-9 (ebk)

For Mary Pat Kunert, with much love.

CONTENTS

ACKNOWLEDGMENTS

Many people have contributed to the writing of this book. Colleagues in the Philosophy Department at Marquette University, Timothy Crockett, Michael Monahan, and Theresa Tobin, read and commented on selected chapters. I thank my colleague Stephen Franzoi of Marquette's Psychology Department for comments on a chapter draft, as well as for other advice. I had the opportunity to comment on the work of John Doris at a conference on "Virtue Ethics and Moral Psychology," held at the University of Denver in October, 2005. I am grateful to him for e-mail exchanges and for sharing his portions of the author meets critics session held at the American Philosophical Association Pacific Division Meetings (Spring 2003), which were later published in *Philosophy and Phenomenological Research* LXXI:3 (November 2005). Colleagues from other institutions read and commented on chapter drafts: thanks are due Marilyn Friedman, Jason Kawall, Christian Miller, and Bill Pollard. Three reviewers on behalf of Routledge, Christian Miller, Linda Zagzebski, and an anonymous referee, read and made invaluable and meticulous comments on the entire manuscript. The book is immeasurably improved thanks to the generosity of all. Needless to say, errors are my own. Chapter 2 consists of reworked material previously published as "Habitual Virtuous Actions and Automaticity," *Ethical Theory and Moral Practice* (November 2006) 9(5): 545–561. It is included here with kind permission of Springer Science and Business Media. Work on the book was begun during my sabbatical year, 2003–2004. I am grateful to Marquette University for providing financial support during this period.

Finally, I would like to thank two people whose support was the *sine qua non* of this book's coming into being: my department chair, James South, and my partner, Mary Pat Kunert. Both of them, especially Mary Pat, put up with me for several years as I wrote it. I dedicate this book to my partner, Mary Pat, with much love.

INTRODUCTION

1. THE SITUATIONIST CHALLENGE TO VIRTUE ETHICS

What is a virtue, and what is the purpose of virtue? Philosophical answers differ. A common response, harking back to Aristotle, is that a virtue is a disposition to act well, and its purpose is to enable us to lead a good life. Virtue on this account allows us to pursue and attain various goods, and thereby to flourish. Another approach, resembling aspects of Hume, sees virtuous dispositions as motivations that are admirable in themselves, apart from any teleological connection they might have with human flourishing. Yet another perspective is pluralistic and non-eudaimonistic. Common to all three conceptions is the notion that virtue is an enduring disposition incorporating practical reason, appropriate motivation, and affect, though they differ in the roles and emphases accorded to each element, and in their positions on the relation of virtue to flourishing. For all three views, virtues constitute important components of personality and, *a fortiori*, character. On these views, the virtues that comprise character are conceived of as temporally stable and regularly manifested in behavior across a wide array of objectively different types of situations. All three accounts provide valuable windows on the nature and purpose of virtue. In recent years, exciting work has been done advancing versions of all three perspectives (Zagzebski 1996; Hursthouse 1999; Foot 2001; Slote 2001; Swanton 2003).

The perspectives on virtue described in the preceding paragraph are central to different versions of what is called "virtue ethics." Virtue ethical theories are those in which virtue is taken to be the central ethical concept in terms of which other ethical concepts, such as the right, are defined. Virtue ethical theories are advanced as stand-alone normative ethical theories, on a par with and as alternatives to deontology and consequentialism. Virtue ethics should be distinguished from virtue theory.[1] Virtue theories seek to explain and justify virtue. Some virtue theories are, but some are not, conjoined with virtue ethics. Some virtue theories are parts of other normative ethical theory-types in which ethical concepts other than virtue are given pride of place. Julia Driver (2001), for example, has advanced a theory of virtue as part of consequentialism, and Kant (1996) has a virtue theory as part of his deontological ethics.

Work in virtue ethics remains largely divorced from empirical psychology, and thus, has been vulnerable to challenge. Impressed with social psychological studies, some philosophers, calling themselves "situationists," are skeptical that there can be enduring personality or character (Harman 1999, 2000, 2003; Doris 1998, 2002, 2005; Merritt 2000).[2] They maintain that personality is far more fragmented than either laypeople or virtue ethicists believe. I will call this group "philosophical situationists," to distinguish them from another group, psychologists who are in the situationist tradition of psychology. As we will see, there are important differences between the claims made by philosophical and psychological situationists, though both groups often refer to the same social psychological studies. According to philosophical situationists, a large number of behavioral studies show that only small numbers of people act in ways consistent with having traits that could be considered virtues in the sense presupposed by the kinds of virtue ethical theories mentioned above (Doris 2002, 6). Consequently, these philosophers argue, it is likely that most people do not have the kinds of traits these virtue ethical theories tell us to have, and, thus, we are unlikely to become the kinds of people they tell us to be (Doris 2002, 6).

In my view, though the specific claims about personality, character, and traits that philosophical situationists make are misguided, their guiding premise is well worth taking seriously. Virtue ethics needs firmer empirical grounding. The aim of this book is to develop a theory of virtue that is grounded in an empirically supported conception of personality, and, *a fortiori*, of character, as coherent and enduring. As I see it, there is good empirical reason to think that personality is coherent and enduring enough to support temporally stable virtues that are regularly manifested in behavior that occurs across objectively different situation-types. In my view, virtue ethics can be empirically grounded, and character in the traditional sense is not an elusive, chimerical ideal. My approach is ecumenical in the sense that I hope to show that virtue as conceptualized by the different versions of virtue ethics mentioned earlier—as an enduring disposition incorporating practical reason, appropriate motivation, and affect—can indeed be grounded by empirical psychology.

To understand the philosophical situationist challenge to virtue ethics and my response to it, we need to explore a debate between personality theorists and social psychologists that took place in the late 1960s and 1970s. Philosophical situationists have been influenced by this debate, and have their own interpretation of its significance—a view that I believe differs from how many psychologists see it.

During the late 1960s and 1970s, situationists in social psychology launched a critique of personality theories with a certain structure—those in which personality, and, *a fortiori*, character, was conceived of as consisting of a panoply of global or robust traits, that is, traits that are both temporally stable and consistently manifested in behavior across a variety of objectively different types of situations (see, e.g., Mischel 1968; Krahé 1990; Ross and Nisbett 1991). According to these personality theories, someone possessing the global trait of honesty should consistently display honest behavior in many objectively different types of situations—when filing her income taxes, in returning lost property, in taking exams, in communicating with others, and so on—and her honesty is temporally stable in the sense that it is reliably manifested in honest behavior over time. Yet, behavioral studies showed that empirical evidence of the existence of global traits was lacking. Studies of honesty in schoolchildren by Hartshorne and May (1928), for example, provided a wealth of data showing that cross-situationally consistent honest behavior is scarce. In these and other situationist experiments, the situations in which behavior was studied were described solely in objective terms, that is, in terms that were accessible to observers, such as the physical or environmental situation of encountering someone slumped over and moaning in a doorway, or finding change in a phone booth, and not in terms of the meanings that the physical situations had for subjects. Convinced by these studies, some psychologists concluded that situations more powerfully influence behavior than do traits, so much so that they were induced to abandon the notion of "trait" as then conceived—as a psychological structure causally implicated in the production of behavior.

Psychologist Walter Mischel, a leader of the situationist critique of personality theory, was among those convinced by Hartshorne and May (1928) and other studies. In his book, Personality and Assessment (1968), Mischel incited a major debate between personality theorists and social psychologists. He took on not only trait theory, but also the other predominant school of psychological thought at the time, psychodynamic or state theory. According to Mischel (1968, 5), trait theory understands personality functioning in terms of stable dispositions, generally regarded as ontologically real, causal forces that produce cross-situationally consistent behavior. Psychodynamic theory, such as Freudianism, understands personality as a product of the interaction of unconscious processes within the individual (Mischel 1968, 7). Mischel (1968, 9) claimed that the value of trait and state approaches lies in how well they facilitate predictions and modifications of behavior. Reviewing a large quantity of research, he concluded that trait and state constructs, as then conceived, are of limited usefulness in understanding human behavior (Mischel 1968, 301). After reviewing the empirical evidence for consistent behavioral manifestations of traits, he concluded: "With the possible exception of intelligence, highly generalized behavioral consistencies have not been demonstrated, and the concept of personality traits as broad response predispositions is thus untenable" (Mischel 1968, 146; quoted in Krahé 1990, 4).

Drawing on numerous pre- and post-1968 social psychological studies, philosophical situationists now make a critique of personality and character that is similar to that begun by Mischel in 1968. At the core of their critique is the assertion that objective situational forces influence behavior far more powerfully than do global traits (Harman 1999, 2000, 2003; Doris 1998, 2002, 2005; and Merritt 2000). Harman, for example, believes these studies show that global traits have little to do with producing behavior and that we have no empirical reason to think that character traits exist (Harman 1999, 316; 2000, 223). We should abandon those versions of virtue ethics that rely on global traits, he contends, in favor of more situationally-based approaches to ethics that have firmer empirical support (see, e.g., Harman 2000, 223–224). Doris (2002, 25, 62ff; 1998, 507) and Merritt (2000, 366, 373–74) argue that, though social psychological studies do not generally warrant ascriptions of global traits, such studies suggest that we are justified in attributing local or situation-specific traits on the basis of narrow behavioral regularities. Doris (2002, 25, 64) believes that evidence against attributions of global traits and in favor of ascriptions of local traits supports a strong fragmentation hypothesis. According to this hypothesis, personality should be conceived of as an evaluatively disintegrated association of situation-specific, local traits. For Doris (2002, 62), these local traits are indexed solely to the objective features of situations, and do not refer to the meanings the situations have for people.3[2] Thus, according to him, local traits are describable as "battlefield physical courage," "storms physical courage," "heights physical courage," etc.

To summarize, philosophical situationists draw on social psychological studies to argue that personality and character are not integrated by the kinds of traits that are traditionally presupposed by virtue ethics. Thus, it is unlikely that most people have the kinds of traits virtue ethics tells us to have, or that most of us can become the kinds of people virtue ethics tells us to be (see Doris 2002, 6). Instead, they contend, social psychological studies show that people generally act in response to influences from the objectively described situations they are in at any given moment.

The contours of this story will be elaborated more fully in chapters to come. For now, suffice it to say that the story can be continued in two ways. One way tracks lines of development in philosophy; the other, advances in psychology. Let us turn to philosophy first.

2. VIRTUE THEORIES THAT EVADE THE SITUATIONIST CRITIQUE

Harman (1999, 327–328) believes that some virtue theories, namely, those that do not conceptualize virtues as global traits, such as Thomson (1996) (and presumably Thomson (1997) which amplifies Thomson 1996), evade the situationist critique. Additionally, inspired by situationist social psychology, Merritt (2000) develops a conception of virtues as local traits that are sustained, not primarily by the force of character, but by social relationships and settings. Finally, Driver (2001) proposes a consequentialist virtue theory that seems to eschew psychology altogether. If these approaches to virtue are empirically adequate by situationist standards, it might be said, there is no need for this volume; that is, there is no need to show that virtues conceived of as global traits can be empirically grounded.

By philosophical situationist lights, these theories could indeed pass empirical muster. Yet there are other grounds on which we can question their adequacy. Of her view, Driver (2001, xxi) writes: "What is unique about the view developed in this book is that it views virtue as having no necessary connection to good psychological states." According to her, a virtue is a trait that "… leads to good consequences systematically," regardless of the scope of the trait—global or local—or of the particular mental state its possessor is in (Driver 2001, xxviii).

Consider some implications of this position. Here is an example I will use for other purposes later in this book. Suppose that Tim wants to be like his father, who is a truly just man in the traditional sense that he is motivated by his sense of justice, and his genuinely just actions hit the target of virtue because they are guided by deliberative excellence. Tim wants to be like his father, and, because of this desire, develops habits of acting in ways that appear to be just. Tim's actions look just and typically maximize good consequences. They thereby satisfy Driver's criterion for virtuous action, even though they are neither motivated by the desire to be just or to act justly nor guided by practical wisdom. Tim would, on my reading of Driver, possess the virtue of justice. But, because Tim is lacking appropriate motivation and practical wisdom, this is nothing like justice in the traditional sense. Things get worse for Driver, for Tim's habitually just actions need not be produced by any coherent psychological structure that endures over time. Tim could even be psychologically disturbed or driven by neurosis to perform apparently just actions, yet, provided that his actions look just and typically maximize good consequences, Driver would consider him to possess the virtue of justice. On Driver's view, the traits that count as virtues are unrecognizable as virtues. This implication of her view seems to me to render it inadequate as a theory of virtue.

Consider now Merritt's (2000) approach. Merritt believes the philosophical situationists are correct in their critique of global traits. If we accept situationist psychology, she thinks, then we must admit that support for situation-specific virtuous dispositions comes largely from external social sources such as particular settings or relationships. She calls these sources of support the "sustaining social contribution to character." She contrasts her conception of virtue as socially sustained, which she calls the "Humean" position, with that of the traditional Aristotelian normative ideal, according to which virtue is sustained through the force of personal character. She calls the latter the ideal of the "motivational self-sufficiency of character" (Merritt 2000, 374).

Merritt recognizes some obstacles to her view, for example, that it is difficult to distinguish internal from external contributions to character, and that there are instances in which people have displayed virtue "... under circumstances where most or all the sources of the sustaining social contribution have completely broken down" (Merritt 2000, 380). She gives as examples of those whose virtue survives the loss of sustaining social structures prisoners of war or prisoners of conscience who have been able to withstand years of hostile captivity (see Merritt 2000, 380). She points to the statistical rarity of such individuals, and writes of their behavior: "... despite its rarity and difficulty it stands for something desirable in the possession of virtue. But what it stand for is, simply, the importance of stability, however that may be secured" (Merritt 2000, 381).

I disagree that what it stands for is the importance of stability alone, no matter the ways in which it is secured. What we admire about prisoners of war who don't break in captivity is precisely their motivational self-sufficiency of character—their independence from the social forces that affect them. What we value is their personal control in forming and maintaining stability of character in ways that enable their characters not only to survive the loss of social sustenance, but also to withstand the forces that would beat character down. We admire those who seem not to be at the mercy of situations, but who are, to some degree, "masters of their fates." They show that we can, within limits, control how situations affect us.

We can and should, as Merritt (2000, 381) maintains, "… take an active, discriminating interest in the climates of social expectation we inhabit." But the real value of attending to the situations that influence us is to strengthen our inner character states, not to form dependencies on external situational props. We need to cultivate our inner states as indemnity against the day when our social sustenance is taken from us—which is not, unfortunately, always statistically rare. When our marriage breaks up, when our loved ones die, when our mortgage is foreclosed in a housing crisis, when a hurricane or tornado or a stock market plunge wipes us out, we need the personal wherewithal to pull through, despite the demise of the social supports that once sustained us. In other words, we need motivational self-sufficiency of character for our daily lives, not just in extreme situations such as hostile captivity.

Ultimately, I believe, Merritt's approach to virtue leads us in a "second best" direction—a direction that has the downside of being unhelpful in precisely those cases in which we need virtue the most—when our social supports give out. Even if Merritt's view passes empirical muster by situationist lights, there is good reason, given the challenges of our daily lives, to continue the search for an adequate empirical basis for virtues conceived of as a subset of global traits. Given that situationist studies are consistent with the existence of small numbers of people who possess global traits, why not study how those traits are formed in an effort to discover general knowledge about global trait cultivation and maintenance? The need for global virtue to help us confront the challenges of daily life makes this an eminently worthwhile undertaking.

Finally, what about Thomson (1996, 1997)? Her views on virtue are parts of an objectivist analysis of non-moral and moral goodness. Thomson (1997, 276–277, 279), distinguishes between first-order and second-order ways of being good. The former are non-moral ways of being good, whereas moral goodness is a type of second-order way of being good. Examples of first-order ways of being good include being "good to," for example, eat, look at, or listen to; being "good for use in," for example, in making cheesecake; being "good at," for example, playing chess; being "good for," for example, planting bulbs; being "good in," for example, a play; and being "good as," for example, Hamlet (see Thomson 1997, 276). Following the use of linguists, Thomson refers to terms such as "to eat," "for use in making cheesecake," etc., as 'adjuncts.' She claims that, in general, "… whenever we predicate an expression of the form 'good plus adjunct', we ascribe a first-order way of being good" (Thomson 1997, 277).

These are all non-moral ways of being good. To understand moral goodness, we need to find out whether acts are generous, brave, just, etc. (see Thomson 1996, 144). To say that X is just, or X is generous, X is brave, and so on, is not, Thomson claims, equivalent to saying X is good plus adjunct. According to her, being just, generous, brave, and so on, are second-order ways of being good that, though not reducible to first-order ways of being good, rest on them in complex ways (see Thomson 1997, 279). To understand how moral goodness rests on non-moral goodness, we need to understand the mental state of the agent when he or she performs a just, generous, brave, and so on, act. Thomson (1996, 145) writes: "Generosity in action has what might be called an intensional connection with the beneficial—and thereby with wants—since an act is generous only if its agent believes that it is good for someone. You don't actually have to succeed in doing what is good for someone; you do have to believe you are doing this." (Yet she apparently changes her view (1997, 281–282), where she makes clear that success, and not just intention, matters to whether an agent has in fact acted virtuously.)

Thomson's analysis of bravery in action parallels her view of generosity in action: "Bravery in action too has an intensional connection with other ways of being good, since an act is brave only if its agent believes that it is, or that its outcome will be, good in some way" (Thomson 1996, 145). Justice is analyzed in similar terms: "... a person's act ... was just only if she believed her act was the according to a person of what she *owed* the person—of what was *due* to the person from her" (Thomson 1996, 146; italics in the original), though justice in action does not have an intensional connection with ways of being good, unlike generosity and bravery in action (see Thomson 1996, 147). These are direct ways in which moral goodness is connected with non-moral goodness.

According to Thomson (1996, 145–146), there are also indirect ways in which moral goodness is connected with non-moral goodness. According to these indirect connections with non-moral goodness, it is good for us, the community, that there are people who are disposed to perform just, brave, or generous actions (see Thomson 1996, 145–147). For example, she claims: "But justice in action has a similar less direct connection with the beneficial. Alice's acting justly is a good sign that she is a just person, that is, that she is disposed to do what she believes she owes to others; and that there are people so disposed in our community is good for us generally—indeed, it is hard to see how we could so much as *be* a community unless a substantial number of us were so disposed" (Thomson 1996, 147; italics in original; see also 1997, 282). The idea is that virtue, as second-order moral goodness, has a general connection with non-moral goodness in the sense that the fact that there are virtuous people is good for us.

It is clear in both Thomson (1996) and (1997) that her account incorporates the notion of dispositions or traits. But Harman (1999, 327–328) claims that it is independent of the idea of traits to some extent. According to Thomson (1997, 280), the notions of a just person and a just act are interdefinable. She belongs to the camp that views the idea of a just act as metaphysically prior, and that of a just person as metaphysically secondary. However, she writes: "But I shall not argue for this idea, since the story I am telling does not rely on it. Given interdefinability, the story I am telling could as well have been told the other way round" (Thomson 1997, 280).

As I read Thomson, the notion of traits is not dispensable; her account relies on it in a significant way. Regarding justice, she holds:

> Justice is proneness to performing just acts; that is, it is proneness to doing what one *owes* to others ... No doubt a particular just act may not on balance be good for people ... But it is better for us that the people among whom we live be just than that they not be just. Indeed, this is not merely better for us, but essential to us, since we can form a community at all—and thereby obtain benefits which are essential to us and which only community can provide—only if a substantial number of those among whom we live are just. (1997, 282; italics in original)

The notion of a trait is not incidental to her view—the link between justice as a moral good and non-moral good, that is, the benefits that justice provides for us, is more clearly forged by persons having the disposition to be just, that is, by their being just persons, not simply by the existence of just acts. But if the notion of a trait is so important to the benefits that virtue can provide for us, it is natural to ask for more information about what a trait is and how traits can be cultivated. What I want to suggest is that Thomson's view is compatible with aspects of the account of traits advanced in this volume such that, should she care to develop her view of traits, a natural tack to take would be similar to the conception of traits presented here. Given that this conception will be presented more fully in later chapters, I advance the compatibility claim about Thomson in the spirit of a promissory note, to be taken on faith until the reader is fully acquainted with the notion of traits I'm developing and in a better position to judge the matter for himself or herself. For the moment, a sketch of this notion of traits and a brief comparison with features of Thomson's view must suffice.

According to the conception of traits advanced here, a trait consists of a stable psychological structure composed of cognitive-affective units, such as beliefs, desires, expectations, values, and self-regulatory strategies and plans. The beliefs of the agent at the time of acting virtuously are part and parcel of her virtuous disposition. In other words, the beliefs that form part of the mental state of the agent when she acts justly, for example, that I owe X to Y and am giving Y her due, are activated cognitive-affective units that form parts of the stable trait of justice—a psychological structure that the agent possesses. Units of this structure can be activated in response to stimuli. For example, seeing an elderly woman being cheated by a sales clerk, the just person would believe that the woman is not getting her due, and would desire to correct the injustice.

As I see it, Thomson's view that the justice of a just action relies in part on the beliefs held by the agent (in addition to its success; see Thomson 1997, 281–282) is consistent with aspects of this structural analysis insofar as both her view and the conception of a trait presented here acknowledge the importance of the agent's beliefs. I'll argue in chapter 4 that these beliefs are shaped by the virtuous agent's motivations such that, should the motivations change, the beliefs would also be affected. Thomson might disagree with this claim. Nevertheless, should she care to unify her analysis of just action with an account of traits, a natural line of development would be to adopt the conception of trait, or something like it, advanced here. This is because the analysis of traits offered here provides an account of the structure and function of traits as they operate in the mental state of the agent. Like Thomson's view, the explanation of traits that I endorse identifies trait components as consisting of beliefs, desires, and other units that function in the mental state of agents. Consequently, the account of traits presented here can be viewed as a possible amplification of claims about virtue made by Thomson.

What can we conclude about Thomson? Even though her theory of virtue evades the philosophical situationist critique in its focus on virtuous action, it falls foul of situationism in its reliance on pronenesses or traits. This reliance, I suggest, is not insignificant. Moreover, given Thomson's stress on the agent's beliefs for the virtuousness of action, her overall approach is not inconsistent with the theory of traits presented here.

To conclude and summarize this section, the verdict for situationist-friendly virtue theories is this. As a virtue theory Driver's (2001) view is, I believe, simply inadequate, since it tells us nothing of interest about the psychological state of the agent and is open to serious objection. Merritt (2000) passes empirical muster by situationist lights, but ignores why we value self-sufficiency of character. We value stability and independence of character because they reflect our personal control over ourselves and the external forces that affect us. We value "self-made" persons and admire their ability to shape themselves and their surroundings. Motivational self-sufficiency of character is valuable indemnity against the day when our social supports fail us. Finally, though features of Thomson's (1996, 1997) view evade the philosophical situationist critique, other aspects rely in significant ways on the idea of traits. Moreover, features of Thomson's theory of virtuous action are compatible with the notion of traits presented here such that, should she care to elaborate her conception of a trait, the account offered here would provide one avenue of development. In short, none of these theories gives us reason to suspend the search for global traits, or to abandon the traditional conception of virtue. Instead, my reading of Merritt (2000) and Thomson (1996, 1997) points us in that direction.

3. DEVELOPMENTS IN PERSONALITY PSYCHOLOGY AFTER MISCHEL (1968)

Now I want to rejoin the story of advances in psychology that took place after Mischel's (1968) critique. For the purposes of this volume, two lines of thought are of interest. The first has to do with post-1968 elaborations of a model of traits called the "five factor model" in personality theory. The second has to do with the subsequent development of Mischel's own work on personality and traits.

Turning first to developments in trait theory, we should note that trait theorists did not simply give up the ghost in light of Mischel's critique. Psychological work on traits is alive and well, and centers on the "five-factor model of personality" (Wiggins 1996). Based on statistical analysis of empirical studies relying on self-report and peer-report data, survey questionnaires, and dictionary entries of trait terms, five traits, called the "big five," have been identified as central to personality: openness, conscientiousness, extraversion, agreeableness, and neuroticism (see John and Srivastava 1999, 105ff; Doris 2002, 67; Mischel, Shoda, and Ayduk 2008, 60–61). Other factors have been identified as correlating with these five, such as sociability and assertiveness with extraversion; trust and compliance with agreeableness; dutifulness and self-discipline with conscientiousness; anxiety and hostility with neuroticism; and curiosity and excitability with openness (see John and Srivastava 1999, 110; Mischel, Shoda, and Ayduk 2008, 60–61). Evidence for the five traits has been widely replicated in both English- and non-English speaking countries; moreover, these traits tend to be relatively stable in adults over time (see Mischel, Shoda, and Ayduk 2008, 61–62).

Why not turn to five factor models in the search for global traits? One reason is methodological: five factor theorists rely on factor analysis of data obtained from various types of paper-and-pencil surveys and dictionary entries of trait terms (see John and Srivastava 1999, 105ff; Mischel, Shoda, and Ayduk 2008, 57; Doris 2002, 67). Though these questionnaires and psychologists' analyses of them are sophisticated, data in favor of the five factors would be strengthened if these methods could be supplemented with behavioral measures. Reliance on paper-and-pencil surveys is one reason Doris (2002, 67) gives for his skepticism about trait theory in psychology. A more serious reason for doubt, in my view, is that five factor theorists disagree on the theoretical underpinnings of the big five traits. Some view trait terms as giving descriptive behavioral summaries; others view traits as psychological or biological structures that provide causal explanations of behavior (see Mischel, Shoda, and Ayduk 2008, 67–68; John and Srivastava 1999, 130; Wiggins 1996). John and Srivastava (1999, 130) write: "... researchers hold a diversity of perspectives on the conceptual status of the Big Five, ranging from purely descriptive concepts to biologically based causal concepts. This diversity may seem to suggest that researchers cannot agree about the definition of the trait concept and that the field is in disarray." They contend, however, that these theoretical variations are not "mutually exclusive" (John and Srivastava 1999, 130). Be that as it may, disagreement about the theoretical status and conceptualization of the big five is significant, not to say daunting, and enough to motivate us to look in a different direction for a theory of global traits that could be useful to virtue ethicists.

The foundations for such a theory can be found in post-1968 developments in Mischel's own work. His 1968 critique of trait and state theories paved the way for more recent work in which he reconceives and unifies trait and state approaches (see Mischel 1973; Shoda and Mischel 1993; Mischel and Shoda 1995; Shoda and Mischel 1996; Shoda and Mischel 1998; Mischel and Shoda 1999; Mischel 1999; Bower 2007, 33–36; Mischel, Shoda, and Ayduk 2008, 402). In this work, Mischel and his collaborator Yuichi Shoda theorize that personality is a cognitive-affective processing system (CAPS). The components of this system, called "social-cognitive units" or "cognitive-affective units," are variables such as beliefs, desires, feelings, goals, expectations, values, and self-regulatory plans. These variables are activated in response to situational features, or in response to internal stimuli, that is, processes or factors internal to the agent, such as her thoughts, imaginings, or practical reasoning. Seeing a person in distress, for example, can make me feel sad, cause me to believe that I should help, activate my desire to help, and set in train plans to offer aid. A similar process might be activated by my simply imagining someone in distress, say, a victim of Hurricane Katrina. Taken together, these components constitute a compassionate response to the real or imagined distress of the other. The repeated activation of sets of such variables over time can result in relatively stable personality structures—traits or dispositions.

According to the CAPS theory of traits, perceptions matter. By this I mean that Mischel and Shoda maintain that people interpret the stimuli they respond to. In other words, they recognize that the objective features of situations have meanings for people, and that this fact is important for understanding personality and behavior. Mischel and Shoda hypothesized that evidence of cross-situational consistency could be found by defining situations in terms of the meanings they have for people rather than in terms of objective features alone (Shoda, Mischel, and Wright 1994, 674; Mischel 1999, 43). It is important to note that this way of defining situations differs from the way in which situations are defined in the social psychological studies on which philosophical situationists draw. In those studies, situations are defined solely in terms of their objective attributes, without taking into account subjects' interpretations of the meanings of the situations. Mischel and Shoda have found empirical evidence of behavioral regularities across objectively different situation-types when situations have similar psychological meanings for subjects. They use the phrase "predictable variability" to refer to their behavioral findings. What they mean by this phrase is that behavior varies predictably across objectively different situation-types that are interpreted in similar terms by the agent. They believe that the predictable variability of the behavior found in their subjects provides evidence in support of personality coherence and stability. As I read their work, "personality coherence" means that from their data we can attribute to agents the existence of different traits that co-exist and constitute the unique personalities of each individual. "Personality stability" means that iterated testing provides evidence that the traits are stable and regularly manifested in behavior over time.

I believe that the CAPS theory of traits provides a promising way of understanding virtue, and is, consequently, significant for philosophers interested in virtue ethics. In chapter one, I present the CAPS theory in more detail, review some of the empirical evidence that has been gathered in its support, and address objections to CAPS traits. I argue that virtues as traditionally conceived can plausibly be considered a subset of CAPS traits. This claim begins my presentation, continued throughout the book, of an empirically adequate theory of virtue.

4. PLAN OF THE BOOK

In chapter 1, "In Search of Global Traits," I sketch out the theory of CAPS traits and present empirical evidence to support it. I believe it is plausible to regard virtues as traditionally conceived as a subset of CAPS traits. This is because virtues and CAPS traits have overlapping properties: both incorporate agents' perceptions and other features of their mental states; both are manifested in behavior that occurs across objectively different situation-types; and both are, or have the potential to become, global. In chapter 1, I also sketch how CAPS traits could be generalized to approximate global traits. This sketch, which is essentially a description of the process of virtue cultivation and vice control, is bolstered by studies from the psychology of prejudice that highlight the kinds of self-regulatory mechanisms that can be used to change personality.

Chapter 1 assumes that we start out with traits that are either local or more extensive, and undertake the process of virtue cultivation and vice control from there. Another avenue for the formation of virtuous dispositions is the habitual performance of virtuous actions. In chapter 2, "Habitual Virtuous Actions and Automaticity," I draw on empirical research on automaticity to argue that habitual virtuous actions can be understood in terms of automatic cognitive processes, that is, processes that occur largely outside of conscious awareness. I contend that explaining habitual virtuous actions in terms of a particular form of automaticity, goal-dependent automaticity, sheds light on how and why such actions are possible, as well as on their rationality. The basic idea is that agents can have mental representations of virtue-relevant goals, such as the goal of being a good parent, or a decent or compassionate person. Encounters with situational features can activate these mental representations outside of the agent's conscious awareness, resulting in virtue-relevant behavior. The repeated activation of representations of virtue-relevant goals in response to situational features eventually results in habitual virtuous actions. Since virtuous dispositions are formed through the habitual performance of virtuous actions, repeated nonconscious goal activation in response to situational features is one way in which virtuous dispositions can be formed. Thus, by the end of chapters 1 and 2, we not only have an empirically adequate conception of traits a subset of which could be virtues, we also have empirically adequate accounts of how virtue can be acquired, either deliberately through self-cultivation, or nonconsciously through habitual virtuous action.

In chapters 3 and 4 I continue the story by looking to psychology for help with another question about virtue: how does virtue help us to live well? Most virtue ethicists think that virtue makes our lives go better. How it does this is elucidated by social intelligence theory in psychology. In chapter 3, "Social Intelligence and Why It Matters," I explain social intelligence theory and make a case for its empirical adequacy. Social intelligence is the knowledge, skills, and abilities that enable us to navigate social life, to interpret and solve the problems life presents, to pursue and achieve our goals at various stages of the lifespan, and, in short, to be effective social participants. A large body of empirical research documents the existence of social intelligence as a form of intelligence that is separate from academic intelligence. This research shows that social intelligence theory is empirically adequate in its own right. However, I bolster this case by arguing that social intelligence research coheres well with other research in personality theory on which this book draws. In chapter 3 I draw on the work of personality theorists Cantor and Kihlstrom (1987) to offer a theory of social intelligence. Finally, I situate social intelligence in a broader conceptual landscape by comparing and contrasting it with neighboring notions, such as social competence, social incompetence, and various interpretations of wisdom.

In chapter 4, "Virtue as Social Intelligence," I argue that virtues are forms of social intelligence. Recognizing that virtues are forms of social intelligence helps to explain how they enable us to live well—they provide us with the knowledge, skills, and sensitivities to live socially and to pursue certain social goals. Social intelligence can be used to pursue any social goal—morally good, morally bad, or neutral. To distinguish virtues from other forms of social intelligence, a claim about the structure of virtue is needed. The claim is that virtues are tightly integrated cognitive-motivational-affective wholes in which the motivations intrinsic to virtues deeply shape the other constituents such that, were the motivations to be removed or replaced, the cognitive elements would change also. Thus, the cognitions that are integral to virtues are not easily or readily separable from the motivational elements. The motivational components of the virtues distinguish them as distinctive forms of social intelligence and separate them from other forms whose cognitive components are shaped by non-virtuous motivations.

By the end of chapter 4, the presentation of the theory of virtue is complete. I hope to have established that there are global traits; that virtues are plausibly regarded as a subset of these traits; that virtue cultivation, both deliberate and through habituation, is an empirically explicable and rational undertaking; that virtue is a form of social intelligence; and that its being a form of social intelligence plausibly helps to explain how virtue enables us to live well. If I am correct, this work shows that virtue, as traditionally conceived, has no shortage of empirical grounding.

In chapter 5, "Philosophical Situationism Revisited," I review with fresh eyes the social psychological studies on which philosophical situationists rely. I believe these studies should be viewed as steps on the way to the deeper and more recent psychological understandings of personality and behavior on which this volume draws. The gist of the argument of chapter 5 is that the situationist studies leave us with perplexing puzzles. To shed light on these puzzles, psychologists, who do not draw the same conclusions from their data as philosophical situationists, generally seek further understanding by investigating subjects' mental states. Psychologists who are puzzled by the results of the situationist studies head in the same general direction as Walter Mischel after his 1968 critique of trait and state theory: they look to the inner psychology of agents, to how agents construe situations and interpret behavior, for a deeper understanding of personality and behavior.

I conclude the book with a look back at the journey taken, and an assessment of the prospects for virtue ethics. Despite the pessimism of philosophical situationists, when all is said and done, the empirical prospects for virtue ethics are good. Virtue ethics is alive and well.

1

IN SEARCH OF GLOBAL TRAITS

1. INTRODUCTION

The aim of this chapter is to advance an empirically supported conception of traits that can help to give virtue, as traditionally conceived, a firm grounding in empirical psychology. The kinds of traits of interest to virtue ethicists should have some of the properties traditionally attributed to virtues. Three of the properties traditionally ascribed to virtues are globality, stability, and reference to the agent's perceptions and other features of her mental states. The traits described here display two of these characteristics —stability and reference to the agent's perspective and mental state—and have the potential for the third—globality. Empirical evidence for these traits has been provided by the work of social-cognitivist psychologists Walter Mischel and Yuichi Shoda.

Mischel and Shoda advance a conception of traits that takes into account the meanings that objective situations have for people. They have found evidence that cross-situational behavioral consistency sufficient to justify trait attributions can be found by considering these meanings as parts of the descriptions of situations. Traits are keyed to the meanings of situations as interpreted by subjects, such as, for example, whether a person finds a situation threatening or irritating, and not solely to the objective features of situations, such as finding a dime in a phone booth, or finding lost change on a table. For Mischel and Shoda, then, situations are identified by the psychological meanings they have for people, as well as by their objective features. Thus, their conception of situations as well as of cross-situational consistency differs from that of situationist psychologists and philosophers.

As I noted in the introduction to this volume, situationists define situations solely in terms of their objective features. By objective features of situations, they mean the physical or environmental characteristics of situations that are accessible to observers and that can be characterized independently of the meanings those features might have for subjects (see Doris 2002, 76). In situationist social psychological studies, experimenters define the kinds of objective situations in which trait-related behavior should be displayed as well as the behavior that counts as manifestations of traits. The perspective of the subject, whose behavior is studied, is not taken into account. Mischel and Shoda thought that studying behavior in situations defined solely in objective terms was the wrong place to look for behavioral consistency. When they redefined situations in terms of the meanings situations have for subjects, they found evidence of behavioral regularities that crossed objectively different situation-types.

In this chapter, I challenge the relevance to virtue ethics of the situationist conception of consistency as regularity in behavior across situations defined solely in objective terms. This is not the kind of behavioral consistency in which virtue ethicists should be interested. Situations have meanings for people, and these meanings are important in assessing whether or not their behavior expresses traits, including traits that can be considered virtues. This important point about traits has been overlooked or minimized by situationist psychologists and philosophers, but not by social-cognitivist psychologists.[1]

In section 2, I explain Mischel and Shoda's social-cognitivist approach and theory of personality. Empirical evidence supporting Mischel and Shoda's conception of traits is discussed in section 3. In section 4, I respond to objections, mainly from Doris (2002, 76–85), to the notion that Mischel-Shoda-type traits have relevance for characterological moral psychology. In section 5, I sketch how these traits, though they might initially be local, can be generalizable across objectively different situation-types, provided that those situation-types have the same or similar meanings for the trait-bearer. Such generalizable traits, I contend, have the potential to be global, at least in some personalities. The sketch of section 5 is also a preliminary exploration of the implications of trait generalizability for virtue development and vice control. I continue this story in section 6 by bringing work in the psychology of prejudice to bear on our understanding of virtue development and vice inhibition. By the end of the chapter, I hope to have presented an empirically adequate conception of traits. Virtues are likely to be a subset of these traits. Descriptions of such traits figure in an empirically plausible sketch of virtue cultivation and vice inhibition. This account of traits is amenable to use in virtue ethical theories that assume that virtues are, or have the potential to be, global.

2. A VIEW FROM SOCIAL-COGNITIVISM

The methodological approach taken by situationist social psychologists has been questioned by social-cognitivist psychologists (see Shoda, Mischel, and Wright 1994; see also Sreenivasan 2002, 58; Kamtekar 2004, 470–473). Social-cognitivists conceptualize personality functioning in terms of the interactions of multiple cognitive and affective processes. These processes, they believe, develop in social and cultural contexts and are activated in social settings (Cervone and Shoda 1999, 4). Social-cognitivists argue that failing to consider the meanings that situations and behavior have for subjects has caused situationist psychologists to overlook trait-relevant behavior (see, for example, Shoda, Mischel, and Wright 1994, 674–675; Mischel 1999, 43–44). For example, subjects and researchers might disagree about what counts as trait-relevant behavior in a given set of circumstances. Behavior that is regarded by researchers as inconsistent across types of situations might not be so regarded by subjects (see also Sreenivasan 2002, 58).

Mischel's (1968) critique of trait and state theories, described in the introduction to this book, presaged more recent social-cognitivist work in which he reconceives and unifies trait and state approaches (see Mischel 1973; Shoda and Mischel 1993; Mischel and Shoda 1995; Shoda and Mischel 1996; Shoda and Mischel 1998; Mischel and Shoda 1999; Mischel 1999, Mischel 2007). Mischel and his collaborator Shoda conceptualize personality as a cognitive-affective processing system (CAPS). The variables of this system, social-cognitive units, consist of beliefs, desires, feelings, goals, expectations, values, and self-regulatory plans, which can be activated either in response to external situational features, or to stimuli internal to the agent, such as her imaginings or practical reasoning. The repeated activation of sets of such variables over time can build relatively stable personality traits.

Mischel and Shoda maintain that people interpret the stimuli they respond to; that is, situations have meanings for people. They believe that how people think and feel about features of situations depends to a certain extent on pre-existing personality variables, such as temperament, as well as on an individual's social learning history. If I am temperamentally disposed to be irritable or fearful, these aspects of my personality influence how I interpret and respond to situations and events.[2] My interpretation of situations and events using categories such as irritating or threatening influences my reactions and reinforces my dispositions. Thus, the traits that I have are shaped both by innate factors as well as by my experiences as a social learner. If this general picture of how personality affects our construals and responses is true, then, to some extent, we influence the quality of the world we inhabit.

Another feature of CAPS traits helps to explain the dynamics of interpretation and response. Mischel and Shoda (1999, 46–53) distinguish between trait structure and the dynamics of trait activation. As I understand their view, the trait is a structure or set of variables that have been frequently activated in response to stimuli. These variables are interconnected in the sense that the activation of one variable can set off or activate others. My belief that another is in need, for example, might activate my desire to offer assistance. Thus, Mischel and Shoda contend that the activation of some variables guides the activation of others. They also hold that the activation of some variables inhibits or constrains the activation of others. For example, my belief that I should help might activate the belief that the other's pride would be wounded by my offer. Other things being equal, this latter belief would typically activate my desire not to cause offense and inhibit or constrain the formulation of plans to help.

Trait structure, then, can be conceptualized as a network of interrelated variables. Different variables can be activated on different occasions. In other words, the dynamics of trait activation vary with variations in activating stimuli. Yet, it makes sense to think that each kind of trait has a distinctive and relatively stable core structure of characteristic variables. What makes compassion distinctive, for example, is being moved to sadness or sorrow by the misfortune of another, believing that one can or should help, and desiring to help. The linkage of these relatively stable variables makes the trait of compassion what it is. The activation of these linked variables produces a compassionate response. This is true even when that response is mitigated by the activation of other variables. That is, a compassionate response remains compassionate even when it has been truncated or constrained, for example, by the belief that the other's pride would be wounded by assistance and the desire not to cause offense.

One final point about the CAPS theory is worth noting. If, for example, Jill consistently reacts fearfully to teasing from playmates whom she perceives as threatening, and Jack consistently reacts aggressively to teasing from playmates whom he perceives as threatening, Mischel and Shoda contend that these facts about their personalities can be described in terms of "if … then" personality profiles or "behavioral signatures" (Mischel 1999, 53; Shoda, Mischel, and Wright 1994, 674; Mischel and Shoda 1999, 207–209). The profiles relate a person's behavior to her construals of situations as they occur over time (Shoda and Mischel 1996,

421–422). The "ifs" are not simply physical stimuli from the external environment, but reflect also the meanings that stimuli have for people. Given sufficient evidence of consistent behavioral reactions under certain psychological conditions, we can typically predict behavior and attribute traits. Given enough evidence, we can say, other things being equal, that "if Jill perceives she is being threatened, she will typically be timid," and "if Jack perceives he is being threatened, he will typically be aggressive," thereby attributing appropriately circumscribed traits of timidity and aggressiveness to each party. Whether Jill reacts timidly and Jack, aggressively, depends on the psychological terms in which each perceives or construes situations, namely, as threatening, and not solely on the situations' objective features.

3. EMPIRICAL SUPPORT FOR CAPS TRAITS

Mischel and his collaborators hypothesize that cross-situational behavioral consistency can be found by examining how people act in situations they perceive as having similar meanings (Shoda, Mischel, and Wright 1994, 674; Mischel 1999, 43). Evidence of this kind of consistency would support the ascription of traits that are generalizable across objectively different types of situations. Mischel and his colleagues have conducted a series of experiments providing evidence in support of various aspects of their hypothesis (see Wright and Mischel 1987; Wright and Mischel 1988; Shoda, Mischel, and Wright 1989; Shoda, Mischel, and Wright 1993; and Shoda, Mischel, and Wright 1994).[3] Among them were studies done at a children's summer camp in New Hampshire (Shoda, Mischel, and Wright 1994). In this research program, eighty-four children were observed during a six week summer session (Shoda, Mischel, and Wright 1994, 77). Researchers distinguished between objective situations that occurred at camp, such as woodworking sessions and cabin meetings, and five different interpersonal situations—(1) positive contact between peers; (2) teasing, provocation, or threatening between peers; (3) praising by adults; (4) warning by adults; and (5) punishing by adults—that occurred in each objective setting. The situations that were the units of psychological study were the interpersonal situations. The interpersonal situations had been selected for study on the basis of previous interviews with the children that enabled researchers to identify the psychological situations that were important for the children at camp (see the description of Mischel and Shoda's work in Mendoza-Denton, Park, and O'Connor 2007, 15). Each of the interpersonal situations incorporated a different combination of two psychologically salient features: whether the interpersonal interaction was initiated by a peer of the subject child or by an adult counselor, and

Table 1.1

Objective Situation	Interpersonal Situations	Psychological Features
E.g., Woodworking	(1) When peer initiated positive contact	Peer, positive
	(2) When peer teased, provoked, or threatened	Peer, negative
	(3) When adult praised	Adult, positive
	(4) When adult warned	Adult, negative
	(5) When adult punished	Adult, negative

whether the interaction was valenced positive or negative (Shoda, Mischel, and Wright 1994, 676–677). Table 1.1 provides examples (excerpted from Shoda, Mischel, and Wright 1994, Table 1, 676).

Subjects encountered each of the five interpersonal situations at least six times (Shoda, Mischel, and Wright 1994, 677).[4] Within each hour of camp activity throughout the six week session, observers recorded the frequency of five types of behavior displayed by subjects in each of the five interpersonal situations. The types of behavior were: (1) verbal aggression (teased, provoked, or threatened); (2) physical aggression (hit, pushed, physically harmed); (3) whined or displayed babyish behavior; (4) complied or gave in; and (5) talked prosocially (Shoda, Mischel, and Wright 1994, 677).

Using this experimental framework, the researchers tested two separate hypotheses. The first hypothesis is that subjects would exhibit stable situation-behavior profiles, expressible as "if … then" statements, that are unique to each individual and provide genuine insight into his or her personality (Shoda, Mischel, and Wright 1994, 677–678). For example, if child A is punished by an adult, she may consistently react with verbal aggression, no matter what the objective setting in which punishment occurs; whereas if child B is punished by an adult, she may typically react with compliance, again across a variety of different types of objective setting. Their behavior is elicited by what the experimenters term the "psychologically salient ingredient" of the interpersonal situation, namely, being punished by an adult. If child A is teased, provoked, or threatened by a peer, she may consistently respond with physical aggression across objective situation-types; whereas if child B is teased, provoked, or threatened by a peer, she may consistently react by whining, again across a variety of objective settings. Again, the behavior, according to the researchers, is elicited by the psychologically salient feature of the interpersonal situation—being teased, provoked, or threatened by a peer. The researchers hypothesized that consistent reactions to different interpersonal situations give insight into an individual's personality. We may infer from child A's consistent reactions that she is verbally and physically more aggressive than child B, who is more inclined to compliance and whining.

The experimenters' second hypothesis is that cross-situational behavioral consistency is a function of the similarity in meanings that different objective situations have for individuals (Shoda, Mischel, and Wright 1994, 681). That is, if child A consistently reacts with verbal aggression to punishment by an adult, no matter what objective setting she is in, her behavioral consistency across the different objective situations is a function of the psychological meaning that the interpersonal experience of being punished has for her. Being punished by an adult is the salient feature of the situation that activates trait-related behavior. Similarly, if child B reacts with compliance to punishment by an adult across different objective situations, that too, is a function of the meaning that punishment by an adult has for him. Consequently, whether people behave consistently across different objective situations depends on the meanings those situations have for them. The researchers tested this hypothesis by compiling comparisons of individuals' consistency in behavior within the same interpersonal situation as it occurred in different objective settings as well as across different interpersonal situations.

Mischel and his colleagues found evidence to support both hypotheses. In support of the first, that stable situation-behavior profiles provide genuine insight into personality, the researchers offered sample situation-behavior profiles of four subjects (Shoda, Mischel, and Wright 1994, 678). Records of verbally aggressive behavior occurring across all five interpersonal situations were presented for four children. Each child had a distinctive profile. For example, child #17's profile was the most stable of the four reported by Shoda, Mischel, and Wright, showing evidence of consistently aggressive behavior across different types of interpersonal situations. He or she exhibited low verbal aggression when teased by a peer, higher verbal aggression when warned by an adult, and very high verbal aggression when punished by an adult. Other children whose data were reported exhibited less stable, yet distinctive profiles.

The experimenters go on to argue that the stable profiles reflect nonrandom aspects of personality and not mere error variance. Shoda, Mischel, and Wright (1994, 680) calculated stability coefficients for the profiles, concluding that for a significant proportion of the children in the sample, the situation-behavior profiles "... tended to constitute a predictable, nonrandom facet of individual differences." That is, the profiles reflect predictable variability in the children's behavior in response to interpersonal situations, and are not measurement errors to be aggregated away (Shoda, Mischel, and Wright 1994, 682). According to the researchers,

Table 1.2

Behavior (verbal aggression) and interpersonal situation	Within the same interpersonal situation	Across different interpersonal situations
Peer teased, provoked	.40 ± .16	.17 ± .13
Adult warned	.33 ± .10	.16 ± .12
Adult punished	.36 ± .10	.15 ± .16
Peer positive contact	.25 ± .16	.07 ± .10
Adult praised	.03 ± .10	.09 ± .10

the stability of these behavioral tendencies over numerous occasions is evidence of the uniqueness of the children's personalities.

In support of the second hypothesis, that cross-situational behavioral consistency is keyed to the meanings interpersonal situations have for people, the researchers compared behavioral consistency within interpersonal situations occurring in different objective settings to behavioral consistency across interpersonal situations. Shoda, Mischel, and Wright (1994, 682) report correlation coefficients for all five behavior types as they occurred across different objective situations for all five types of interpersonal situations. The correlation coefficients for verbal aggression are lited in Table 1.2 (excerpted from Shoda, Mischel, and Wright 1994, Table 3, 682).

The first entry in the column on the left indicates that the mean correlation of verbally aggressive behavior in response to being teased or provoked by a peer within the same type of interpersonal situation as it occurred in different objective situations was .40 with an estimated error of .16. The first entry in the column at the right indicates that the mean correlation of verbally aggressive behavior in response to being teased or provoked by a peer in each of the four other interpersonal situations (being warned by an adult, being punished by an adult, being praised by an adult, or having positive peer contact) was .17 with an estimated error of .13.

As the correlation coefficients indicate, for all of the interpersonal situations except the "adult praised" condition, the likelihood of verbally aggressive behavior occurring in response to the same type of interpersonal situation across different types of objective situations was higher than the likelihood of its occurrence across different types of interpersonal situations. This is evidence that behavioral consistency is a function of the perceived meanings of situations. Further support for this claim is provided by the researchers' finding that as the number of shared psychological features of interpersonal situations decreased, the consistency of individual differences in behavior also decreased (Shoda,

Mischel, and Wright 1994, 681–682). As the researchers report, within interpersonal situations that shared at least two common features (e.g., when warned by an adult and when punished by an adult), the mean consistency in individual differences in verbal aggression was .28. Between two different situations that shared only two features, the mean consistency in individual differences in verbal aggression was .25. When two psychological situations shared only one common feature, the mean consistency was .15. When the situations shared no common features, the mean consistency was .06.

These findings are of philosophical interest. Consistent behavioral reactions in response to similarly perceived interpersonal situations that occur across different objective settings ground attributions of traits that are in principle generalizable across objectively different situation-types. Before exploring trait generalizability, however, objections need to be addressed.

4. OBJECTIONS TO CAPS TRAITS

Doris is, of course, aware of Mischel and Shoda's conception of traits. He seems to admit that their findings show something real about personality coherence, but questions whether this coherence is of interest to characterological moral psychology (Doris 2002, 77–78). His point is that findings of behavioral consistency across psychologically defined situations should not assuage concerns about the lack of behavioral consistency across situations defined in objective terms (Doris 2002, 78). He illustrates his perspective by constructing a "personological fantasy" (Doris 2002, 78–84).

The fantasy is based on the behavior and remarks of Eisuke Shigekawa. Climbing Mount Everest in the spring of 1996, Shigekawa and his team passed two dying climbers without stopping to help. Commenting on this omission, Shigekawa remarked: "Above 8,000 meters is not a place where people can afford morality" (quoted in Doris 2002, 78). Based on this incident, Doris asks us to imagine a climber for whom compassion is altitude-indexed: below 8,000 meters, she consistently stops to help those in distress; above 8,000 meters, she consistently does not. Doris suggests that we can attribute a trait to her, called altitude-indexed compassion, or "aipassion" for short. Aipassion reliably results in compassionate behavior below 8,000 meters and in incompassionate behavior above. The climber, then, is consistently aipassionate.

Doris (2002, 80) remarks: "Consistency is relative. Talk of consistency or inconsistency *simpliciter* is meaningless, and inconsistency relative to one standard may be consistency relative to another." The kind of consistency that is interesting for characterological moral psychology, he thinks, is consistency relative to the objective features of situations and to traditional moral traits.

I find this example puzzling as a commentary on Mischel and Shoda's conception of traits. The empirical work reviewed in section 3 carefully documents, for each child, the frequency of types of behavior that he or she performed in numerous interpersonal situations during the course of a six week summer session at camp. Based on the frequency of occurrences of a specific type of behavior performed by a child, we can speak of her in traditional trait terms— that is, in terms that have traditionally been used in our common vocabulary to name dispositions that we think produce that type of behavior. In fact, the descriptions of the interpersonal situations that were selected for study were derived from interviews with the children in which they described the behavior of their peers in traditional trait terms, for example, "When Johnny is teased about his glasses, he's aggressive" (Mendoza-Denton, Park, and O'Connor 2007, 215). To the best of my knowledge, nowhere in Mischel and Shoda's work do they suggest that we are justified in inventing a new trait term to apply to two different types of behavioral regularities that an individual displays. In other words, I do not believe that Mischel and Shoda, in an effort to manufacture consistency where none exists, would invent a term such as "aipassion" and claim that this is the trait responsible for the climber's compassionate behavior below 8,000 meters and incompassionate behavior above. What would be the empirical basis for unifying regularities in her two different types of behavior under the umbrella of a single, newly minted trait term?

Mischel and Shoda would claim, I believe, that the climber shows regularities in one type of behavior, namely helping behavior, at altitudes below 8,000 meters, and regularities in another type of behavior, namely omissions of helping behavior, above. They would explain these behavioral differences by reference to differences in her subjective construals of the objective features of the situations of persons in distress above and below 8,000 meters.

This approach, it seems to me, would be right. Lacking a difference in the objective situations of those in distress above and below 8,000 meters, the differences in the climber's behavior at the different altitudes must be a function of her subjective perspective, that is, of the differences in meaning that seeing persons in distress has for her at different altitudes. One might contend that there are objective differences in the situations of those in distress at high and lower altitudes.[5] For example, it is harder at higher altitudes to get those in need down to hospitals where they could receive medical care, and the lives of those providing assistance could be endangered in attempts to render aid. Furthermore, one might argue that those climbing at higher altitudes have voluntarily put themselves at risk, which could limit duties others have to assist them should danger arise. These objective differences, however, are susceptible to different subjective interpretations. A climber might admit these objective differences, yet make the subjective judgment that it is her duty to help. Alternatively, one might invoke subjective judgments about altitude-based objective differences to justify a lack of compassionate behavior at higher altitudes. The point is that objective differences in circumstances have subjective meanings for people, and these meanings influence behavior. Doris's example, I believe, illustrates the social-cognitivist's point that explaining behavioral regularities requires taking into account the meanings that objective circumstances have for people.

Here is another concern. Would we really want to say that our climber, for example, is truly compassionate below 8,000 meters while acknowledging that this trait stops operating above 8,000? Isn't this altitude-indexed behavior too odd to warrant the belief that genuine compassion is producing it? Our climber seems deeply out of touch with common norms for the expression of trait-relevant behavior.

In the case of our climber, I would want to say that she is indeed compassionate below 8,000 meters. Here is why. We have no reason to think that her compassion below 8,000 meters is not genuinely felt sorrow for the plight of another, nor that, at altitudes above, she ceases to perceive and feel in the way compassion requires. We don't even have reason to believe that her subjective construals of when compassion is required are idiosyncratic and diverge wildly from commonly accepted norms that regulate appropriate expressions of compassion. Like Shigekawa, she apparently thinks that compassion is out of place at very high altitudes. Presumably, Shigekawa had a reason for thinking this—perhaps that at such high altitudes, one's own survival is paramount and one cannot expend energy on helping others. One might criticize this explanation of Shigekawa's (and our climber's) altitude-indexed compassion, but one can surely understand it—it is intelligible. The only thing that is idiosyncratic about our imaginary climber is that her compassion is so precisely indexed. But her compassion is indexed by hypothesis; the example does not come from real life.

An objector could now introduce a panoply of experiments on real-life people studying the effects of trivial environmental factors, such as noise level, room temperature, and fragrances, on helping behavior (see Carlson, Charlin, and Miller 1988, and Schaller and Cialdini 1990 for overviews).[6] These factors apparently affect mood, and thus, behavior, but below the level of the agent's conscious awareness. That is, people are generally unaware that such factors affect their behavior. Suppose that when Jenny smells a pleasing aroma she consistently reacts with compassion to persons undergoing a certain kind of plight, yet, when the fragrance is absent, she fails to react compassionately when confronted with the same kind of situation. Wouldn't we think that, if her compassion were indeed robust, she would react compassionately whether or not she smelled the bouquet?

I consider the mood effect studies in chapter 5. As we'll see, I'm skeptical that they're relevant for virtue theory. For now, however, suffice it to say that, if these studies do challenge virtue theory, and thus, virtue ethics, they also call into question any theory of ethics that presupposes that ethical action is affected only by conscious deliberation. In other words, if the effects of trivial factors on behavior are as pervasive as the mood effect studies seem to indicate, then rule-governed behavior and utility-maximizing behavior, as well as trait-expressive behavior, should be affected. If the mood effect studies are relevant to ethics at all, their relevance consists in the fact that they raise the question of the extent, if any, to which an ethical theory should be expected to take account of the effects of nonconscious factors on behavior.

For now, however, let us continue with further objections to CAPS traits. Doris (2002, 85) expresses two further concerns about Mischel and Shoda's approach: "First is the empirical problem of identifying behavioral patterns indicative of coherence. Second is the conceptual problem of adducing affinities between this newfound coherence and traditional moral trait taxonomies."

Empirical studies, including that reviewed earlier, address Doris's first concern.[7] His second concern is also offset by the empirical studies, which track behaviors linked with aggression, withdrawal, and compliance in children—traits associated with traditional trait taxonomies in personality theory. I see no reason, either theoretical or empirical, why Mischel and Shoda's theory could not be tested with respect to traits more relevant to virtue ethics, such as honesty or compassion.[8]

Another remark by Doris is worth mentioning. He believes that CAPS traits track narrow behavioral regularities, and thus, are superficially similar to the local traits he posits to explain the behavioral regularities found in some social psychological experiments (Doris 2002, 77). He acknowledges, of course, that Mischel and Shoda's conception of a trait is embedded in a conception of personality as a cognitive-affective system (Doris 2002, 77). However, as Doris knows, his notion of local traits differs from Mischel and Shoda's in a very important respect. For Doris, local trait ascriptions are warranted on the basis of narrow behavioral regularities that are keyed to the objective features of situations. This is evident in how local traits are described, as for example, "office-party-sociability," or "answer-key-honesty." These traits are always relativized to situations described in purely objective terms.

By contrast, CAPS traits are ascribable on the basis of behavioral regularities that are indexed to the psychologically salient features of situations, such as whether a subject perceives a situation as irritating or threatening. Since the same or similar psychological features can be elicited for a subject by objectively different types of situations, behavioral consistency, too, can span objective situation-types. Thus, unlike Doris's traits, CAPS traits are not narrowly relative to the objective features of situations, but can be manifested in behavioral consistencies across objectively different situation-types.

It is possible that persons possess CAPS traits that are local. Local CAPS traits could be narrowly keyed to a person's subjective construals of objective situations, yet not be generalized across other objective situations that could plausibly be construed in similar subjective terms. For example, Sally might be on the receiving end of what an observer would perceive as the same kind of demeaning treatment from her father and from a stranger. It is possible for Sally to interpret the treatment from the stranger as demeaning, yet construe differently what an observer would regard as objectively the same kind of treatment—perhaps degrading remarks—from her father. An observer might reasonably interpret such remarks from both the stranger and the father as forms of abuse. But Sally might perceive such treatment from her father as his way of teasing her; she doesn't think he "means anything by it." In response to her father's treatment, she could develop a local trait of docility-toward-her-father that that she does not generalize to situations of demeaning treatment involving strangers because she does not interpret their behavior in the same way as she construes her father's. As I see it, there is nothing to prevent such subjectively indexed traits from remaining local in some personalities, though subjectively indexed traits can also, I maintain, be generalized across objective situation-types that have the same or similar meanings for a person.

Another possible objection to CAPS traits is that empirical evidence for these traits was found by studying children. If we are interested in traits a subset of which could be virtues, wouldn't stronger empirical evidence be furnished by studies done with adults?

The Shoda, Mischel, and Wright (1994) studies supply evidence, even in a population of children, of behavioral consistencies that make sense—behavior varies consistently and predictably in response to the perceived meanings of situations. It is plausible to think that this would be as true of adult subjects as it is of children. In fact, it makes sense to think that psychologically indexed trait-relevant behavioral consistencies would be more pronounced in adult subjects than in children, since adults are generally more aware of the interpersonal dynamics of situations. For both children and adults, I believe, indexing trait-relevant behavior to the meanings of situations is looking in the right direction for evidence of cross-situational behavioral consistency and thus, of the existence of traits.

An interesting study by Lord (1982) supports this contention for the case of adults. He writes: "An individual will behave consistently across situations he or she perceives as similar. But what dimensions of similarity do individuals use" (Lord, 1982, 1076)? To answer this question, he tested eight different similarity assessment measures to see how well they predicted cross-situational consistency in conscientious behavior. Three assessment techniques were successful predictors of cross-situationally consistent conscientious behavior in Lord's subjects: goal satisfaction ratings, self-template matches, and template-template matches (see Lord 1982, 1084).[9]

Here is a word of explanation about each method (see Lord 1982, 1078). The idea behind goal satisfaction ratings is that individuals might decide that situations are similar according to how well the situations enable them to satisfy important goals. Thus, goal satisfaction ratings can serve as indexes of perceived similarity between situations, and a person's behavior across those situations can be tested for consistency. What about self-template matches? A template, as I understand it, is a conception of a certain type of situation. Self-template matching relies on the idea that situations are sometimes perceived in terms of the dispositions and characteristics of the persons typically found in them. Thus, a person might perceive certain kinds of situations according to templates in which those situations call for a certain kind of behavior, such as conscientiousness, perceive herself as a conscientious person, and behave conscientiously in those situations. Situations calling for conscientiousness can vary in their objective descriptions. Someone might regard conscientiousness as called for in situations involving taking a friend to the airport in time for a flight, performing tasks for elderly relatives, being on time for appointments, etc. A person can be consistently conscientious in these objectively different types of situations because she regards herself as conscientious and views objectively different situations in similar terms—as calling for conscientious behavior. Template-template matching relies on the idea that a person's template for one type of objective situation might be similar in some respects to that of an objectively different type of situation. Consistency of behavior across objectively different situations having similar templates can be tested. For example, a person might have a situation template for being in church that requires quiet behavior, and a situation-template for listening to a lecture that also calls for quiet behavior. A person need not see herself as quiet in order to behave quietly in these situations, though she might regard herself as having another trait, such as respect for others, which would lead to quiet behavior in such circumstances.[10] All three of these methods are idiographic; that is, all three draw on the individual's own perceptions of situational similarity, and all three methods yielded statistically respectable predictions of cross-situationally consistent behavior. The results of Lord's approach, as I read them, lend credence to the social-cognitivist view that attention must be paid to how individuals interpret situations in order to understand personality and behavior.

Contrary to Doris's view, I believe that Mischel and Shoda's social-cognitivist view affords exactly the kind of insight into personality functioning that is of interest to philosophical studies of virtue and character. Their approach of charting individual differences in behavioral regularities in response to the psychologically salient features of situations gives us a place to look for evidence of cross-situationally consistent behavior. Such evidence grounds attributions of the kinds of traits that are likely to be considered virtues.

5. LOCAL TRAIT GENERALIZABILITY, VIRTUE DEVELOPMENT, AND VICE CONTROL: A PRELIMINARY SKETCH

It is plausible to understand traditional virtues as a subset of CAPS traits. CAPS traits are activated in response to agents' subjective construals of the objective features of situations, are temporally stable, and have been manifested in cross-situationally consistent behavior. Virtues as traditionally conceived are thought to have similar properties. In addition, the theoretical structures that have been posited to explain CAPS traits are similar to how philosophers have usually thought of the structure of virtuous dispositions: as relatively stable configurations of characteristic types of thoughts, motivations, and affective reactions, standing "on call" and ready to be activated in response to the appropriate stimuli. Could CAPS traits be generalizable across different objective situation-types, and thereby approach globality in some personalities?

To explain how CAPS traits could be generalizable across objective situation-types, consider how CAPS explains someone with an irritable personality. If this person is irritable, her disposition, perhaps abetted by innate biological factors such as temperament, has been built up over time through repeated encounters with stimuli that have made her prone to irritability. A structure for the trait of irritability, consisting of thoughts, affects, and representations of plans, strategies, and values, stands on-line and "on call," ready to be activated through encounters with external stimuli or even through other internal stimuli, such as thoughts or imaginings. Because of the existence of this structure, she is predisposed to irritable reactions and behavior. She is likely to select and construe certain features of her environment as irritants and to react accordingly. When she does in fact become irritated in response to situational features, perhaps as a reaction to a shop clerk's offhand remark, which she interprets as rude, selected units in the processing structure become activated. These units—thoughts, such as "that was uncalled for;" affects, such as feelings of anger and annoyance; and strategies, such as "I'll show him; I'll complain to the manager," come into play. These units form the processing dynamic of the activated trait in response to the specific encounter.

Given this description, we can see how traits can become generalized across different types of objective situations that a person construes in similar subjective terms. Such generalized traits can approximate global traits in some personalities. That is, on the CAPS model, if a trait starts out by being narrow and local, perhaps as a response to a subjective interpretation of one type of objective situation or encounter, it need not remain confined to the same type of objective situation, but can be generalized across objectively different situation-types that have the same or similar meanings for the trait-bearer. If an offhand remark by a store clerk can be perceived as rude, so can a casual comment by a friend over lunch, by the postman, by the receptionist in a doctor's office, and so on. In other words, the meanings that trigger trait-based responses generalize across objective situation-types. Meanings are not ineluctably confined to the same types of objective situations.

To see this, consider the many types of objectively different situations that one might perceive as annoying, and in which the traits of irritability or anger might be activated. Or, consider the many types of objectively different situations that one might perceive as threatening, and in which fear might be elicited. If repeated encounters with stimuli perceived as annoying or threatening build up relatively stable trait structures over time, then the traits that are activated in various types of objective situations are the same traits. That is, my irritability is the same trait, though elicited across various types of objectively different situations. Different variables or units of the trait are activated in response to specific situational encounters, but all of the units are parts of a larger, stable trait structure that is an enduring part of my personality. In other words, trait structure remains the same, but the dynamics of trait activation vary with variations in stimuli. If this picture is correct, there is no need to posit local traits that are indexed to the objective features of situations, such as "office-party-sociability," or "exam-taking-honesty." Instead, there are sociability and honesty, activated in response to a person's subjective construals of similarities among the different objective situations she encounters. On this view, personality is more unified and coherent than is likely for the fragmented conception of personality entailed by positing local traits that are indexed to narrowly described objective features of situations.

Sometimes, perhaps often, the process by which traits become generalized across situation-types is not salient to the agent. In other words, it is possible that our irritable woman has become that way without really noticing how entrenched and pervasive that trait has become, how deeply and prominently a part of her personality it is. Being irritable has become habitual for her—an automatic or nonconscious way in which she perceives and reacts to the world. As practical reasoners, however, we can evaluate and, within limits, shape who we are.[11] We have the ability to reflectively observe the meanings we attribute to situations and how we react to them. Not only can we observe, we can, within limits, control how things seem to us and how situations affect us. We can bring entrenched habits and tendencies to conscious awareness and evaluate and try to revise them.

Suppose that one day our irritable woman is told by a friend, "You really have become an angry person. You don't like anything or anyone." Reflecting on these comments, the irritable one realizes their truth. She does not like this fact about herself. She resolves to change, begins observing when she becomes irritable, and starts asking herself why. Perhaps she gets some therapy to help her ferret out the deeper causes of her chronic negativity. With work, she can try to change, by reinterpreting the situational cues that generate her irritability and acknowledging and controlling her prickly impulses. She can work to develop a different perspective on the things that annoy her, changing her outlook in order to modulate her reactions. In the language of the psychological processing of stimuli, we can say that she is working to ensure that some variables in her processing structure for irritability do not become activated; she is changing her processing dynamics. In the language of social intelligence, explored in chapters 3 and 4 of this volume, she is monitoring her perceptions, judgments, and reactions and working to change the interpretative framework that gives rise to them.

How should we think about the cultivation of moral virtue in light of the framework provided by CAPS traits? Here is a preliminary sketch. Suppose that I show great compassion, but only in certain cases, perhaps those involving small, cuddly animals. My compassion is domain-dependent. I wish that I could extend my compassion to the domain of people and take as my goal becoming a more globally compassionate person. If the foregoing argument is correct, I can attempt to generalize my compassion through self-scrutiny and practical reason. I begin to monitor and evaluate my compassionate reactions, examining them with the plan of self-development. First, I ask myself why I show compassion only toward small animals. What is it about them that elicits this response? Through reflection, I ascertain that I perceive them as vulnerable, and this perception of vulnerability evokes compassionate feelings in me. I then ask myself why I do not perceive the vulnerabilities of fellow humans. After all, they, too, are sometimes in distress, and in need of help. I work to become more aware of common human vulnerabilities. Perhaps through imaginative dwelling on the plights of those in need, I try to generate feelings of compassion. I reflect on and seek to remove or overcome factors that might inhibit my compassionate response, such as the fear of being rebuffed or rejected. I educate myself to become more aware of compassion-eliciting circumstances, to pick up on cues from others that might reveal distress. I try to habituate myself to perceive these cues and react compassionately. This is not an easy process. It requires introspection and the deliberate training of my capacities for affect, perception, and response. Instilling in myself the emotional reactions required for compassion could be especially difficult. Perhaps, given my temperament and social learning history, some emotions are unavailable to me. In other words, in some areas, I could be permanently repressed. If so, I might be able to experience some virtues only imperfectly, if at all. The point, however, is that this or a similar process of self-regulation could in principle be used to cultivate virtues and extend them across domains. In this way, persons whose virtues may initially be manifested solely in narrow behavioral regularities that are keyed to the perceived meanings of certain kinds of objective situation-types can attempt to extend their virtues across objectively different types of situations.

6. VIRTUE CULTIVATION AND VICE INHIBITION: LESSONS FROM THE PSYCHOLOGY OF PREJUDICE[12]

The process of virtue development sketched here entails two aspects: virtue cultivation and vice inhibition. Can it actually be done? An impressive array of research on stereotypes from the psychology of prejudice suggests that it can. Like traits, stereotypes are deep-seated psychological constructs whose activation often occurs automatically and outside of the agent's conscious awareness. That is, certain features of a target, such as gender characteristics or skin color, can activate a stereotype and influence behavior without our knowing it.

Can stereotype activation be prevented, interrupted, or inhibited? Some evidence suggests that it can (see Devine 1989; Gilbert and Hixon 1991; Monteith 1993; Fazio, Jackson, Dutton, and Williams 1995; Blair and Banaji 1996; Lepore and Brown 1997; Sinclair and Kunda 1997; Macrae, Bodenhausen, and Milne 1998; Devine and Monteith 1999; Devine, Plant, and Buswell 2000). Here I draw on the work of Patricia Devine and Margo J. Monteith, whose research on stereotype activation and control is not only interesting in its own right but is also suggestive in its possible implications for trait winnowing and cultivation. If stereotype activation can be inhibited through self-regulatory motivations and intentions, then trait activation might be similarly controlled.

Devine and Monteith (1999) describe a model of self-regulatory control by means of which stereotype activation can be repeatedly interrupted, and the stereotype eventually replaced with nonprejudiced patterns of responding. They introduce their model with the example of Paula, who has a stereotypic response to a fellow shopper in a grocery store. The discrepancy between her response and her internalized standards rejecting prejudice causes Paula to feel guilty about her lapse (Monteith 1993, 470; Devine, Plant, and Buswell 2000, 192). According to Devine and Monteith (1999, 351), the fact that Paula has felt guilty and has considered her response for even a few seconds is important for decreasing the likelihood that she will make the same kind of prejudiced response in the future. Paula's experience builds an association between the store environment, her stereotypic inference, and her experienced guilt. Because of these associations, Devine and Monteith (1999, 351–352) predict that Paula should think twice the next time a stereotypic response is possible.

Paula's plight is similar to that of the irritable woman described in the previous section. Both have identified tendencies in themselves that they condemn and wish to be rid of. These tendencies are deep-seated cognitive-affective propensities whose activation occurs outside of their conscious awareness. Paula, before she knows it, has a stereotypic reaction to members of minority groups. Our irritable woman finds herself becoming irritated almost constantly, and does not know why. Both women seek to inhibit or control these negative propensities, and have internalized alternative standards and personal beliefs about more appropriate attitudes and behavior. Both are motivated to enact these standards and beliefs. Both catch themselves when backsliding into inappropriate behavior and experience negative self-directed affect, such as guilt and shame, when lapses occur.

Devine likens the process of stereotype inhibition to that of breaking a bad habit—of trying to replace negative responses with self-controlled, positive reactions that accord with an agent's personal standards and beliefs (Devine 1989, 15; see also Devine, Plant, and Buswell 2000). To successfully kick the habit, an individual must: "... (a) initially decide to stop the old behavior; (b) remember the resolution; and (c) try repeatedly and decide repeatedly to eliminate the habit ... In addition, the individual must develop a new cognitive (attitudinal and belief) structure that is consistent with the newly determined pattern of responses" (Devine 1989, 15). Those who wish to kick their habit, that is, those who have internalized nonprejudiced standards and are motivated to act accordingly, receive external cues or triggers that activate their previously internalized stereotype. They then experience guilt over the discrepancy between their standards and their response. Awareness of the discrepancy not only causes self-directed negative affect, it also elicits heightened self-focused attention and subsequent efforts to control unwanted responses (see Devine and Monteith 1999, 352–353).

Devine and Monteith explain more specifically how control might be gained over automatically generated responses by extrapolating from a neuropsychological model of learning and motivation developed by J. A. Gray (Devine and Monteith 1999, 353; Monteith, 470–471; 477; Gray and McNaughton 2000). According to Gray's model, awareness of a discrepant response should activate a behavioral inhibition system (BIS). BIS activation results in increased arousal and an automatic, momentary interruption of behavior. Attention is then turned to the behavioral sequence that resulted in the discrepant response so the person can determine what went wrong. The individual attempts to identify environmental stimuli that were present when the discrepant response occurred. Ideally, an association is created among cues present when the discrepant response occurred, the response itself, and negative affective consequences, such as guilt. In this way, through a process that has been called "retrospective reflection," cues for punishment (guilt) can be established (see Devine and Monteith, 353).

The operation of BIS and the establishment of cues for punishment are crucial for kicking the prejudice habit. When automatic stereotype activation occurs on subsequent occasions and punishment cues have been established, the presence of similar cues should serve as a warning signal that activates BIS, thereby resulting in increased arousal and a slowing of ongoing behavior. This allows the person to proceed more carefully, bringing personal beliefs to mind as a basis for controlled, rather than automatic, responses to stereotype activation. As Devine and Monteith summarize: "Through behavioral inhibition, the automatic processing that would otherwise give rise to a prejudiced response is disrupted, and the individual has the opportunity to generate a nonprejudiced response based on controlled processing … Control is exerted both in the interruption of stereotype activity and in the generation of a personally acceptable response" (1999, 353).

Work in the psychology of prejudice has focused on processes for controlling behavioral responses to stereotype activation; on processes for interrupting stereotype activation, as in the self-regulation model just described; and, most recently, on how stereotype activation might be prevented entirely (Devine and Monteith, 1999, 354). Devine and Monteith suggest that the long-term, practiced inhibition of stereotype activation and replacement with controlled responses could result in the prevention of stereotype activation and the increasingly frequent activation of and reliance on nonprejudiced responding (Devine and Monteith, 354). In other words, the process they describe shows how suitably motivated individuals can break free of bad habits of prejudice and inculcate good habits of acting in accordance with personal standards and beliefs.

If the process of trait activation functions like that of stereotype activation, Devine and Monteith's self-regulatory model shows that there may be hope for our irritable woman as well as for the person who seeks to extend her compassion into different domains. If these people are appropriately motivated to change, they can take advantage of the BIS. They can search for environmental cues that trigger responses discrepant from their newfound standards of behavior in efforts to establish an association between cues, discrepant responses, and guilt. Repeated activations of the BIS and the use of punishment cues can help them to inhibit and eventually prevent the discrepant responses they seek to overcome, replacing them with controlled responses crafted on the basis of personal beliefs, perhaps about the preferability of patience and kindness to irritability, or the need for compassion to replace indifference or callous disregard and extend to all domains of life.

Whatever specific psychological processes are involved, the point is that the self-regulatory model of stereotype control, backed by empirical research, shows how personality change is possible, and provides indirect, yet plausible support for the kind of self-shaping sketched earlier. If it is possible to shape one's traits by repeatedly inhibiting negative trait tendencies and replacing them with positive, controlled responses that eventually result in old trait structures being replaced with new, more desirable ones, and similar self-regulation can be used to extend behavior manifesting existing positive traits into new domains, then virtuous development across domains is possible. Though our virtues might start out by being local, they need not remain so.

7. CONCLUSION

To conclude, let me summarize the gist of this chapter. The aim of the chapter was primarily to develop the empirically grounded CAPS conception of traits. In the chapter's introduction and first section, I sketched the social-cognitivist approach to situations and cross-situational consistency and contrasted it with the approach taken by situationists. Whereas situationists look for evidence of global traits in behavioral regularities across objectively different situation-types, social-cognitivists stress the importance that the meanings of situations have for people, and claim that evidence of personality coherence can be found by paying attention to those meanings. I've sketched Mischel and Shoda's CAPS conception of traits that are indexed to the meanings that situations have for people, and have reviewed empirical evidence in support of it. These traits, I've argued, are generalizable across objectively different situation-types and thus, have the potential to be global. Virtues, I believe, can plausibly be considered traits of this type. Drawing on empirical research on stereotypes, a construct that is very similar to traits, I've sketched a model of self-regulatory trait development. This model suggests that it is possible, with effort, to inhibit and control negative traits and cultivate and extend desired ones. The model is a plausible interpretation of how virtue might be cultivated and vice, controlled.

The CAPS conception of traits is empirically adequate, and is amenable to virtue ethical theories in which virtues are either assumed to be global or to have the potential for globality. Moreover, the sketch of self-regulatory trait development is an empirically plausible story of how virtue cultivation and vice inhibition can occur. I believe that the story presented in this chapter provides a rejoinder to the recent situationist challenge to virtue ethics.

The story doesn't end here. The cultivation of virtue described in the last two sections is a very deliberate process, requiring conscious self-regulation. There is another way in which virtue is developed—through the performance of habitual virtuous actions. Unlike the process of virtue cultivation sketched in this chapter, the development of virtue through habit is not entirely deliberate, and is often not salient to the agent's conscious awareness. Yet, as I argue in the next chapter, habitual virtuous actions are often rational and goal-directed. These claims, too, are supported by empirical psychology.

2

HABITUAL VIRTUOUS ACTIONS AND AUTOMATICITY

1. INTRODUCTION

In chapter 1, I argued that empirical psychology provides evidence for the existence of traits that give rise to behavioral regularities that cross objectively different situation-types. Virtues can plausibly be considered a subset of these traits. In the last sections of chapter 1, I sketched one way in which character can be shaped—through deliberate virtue cultivation and vice inhibition. In this chapter, I explore another aspect of character formation. Virtues can be acquired by performing habitual virtuous actions. Here I argue that one can understand habitual virtuous actions as rational actions that are directed to achieving virtue-relevant goals. The basic picture is that a mature agent might have a virtue-relevant goal, such as being a good parent, or promoting peace, and build up virtues through repeatedly acting in ways that advance those goals. There is much more, of course, to this story.

Habitual virtuous actions are performed repeatedly and automatically, that is, apparently without thinking. In this chapter, I bring recent work on automaticity in cognitive and social psychology to bear on our understanding of habitual virtuous actions. In section 2, I offer a brief primer on automaticity, focusing mainly on one form, goal-dependent automaticity. Goal-dependent automaticity, I believe, furnishes a promising empirical framework for understanding habitual virtuous actions, including how and why such actions can occur across many objectively different situation-types. In section 3, I examine recent accounts of habitual action and habitual virtuous action advanced by Pollard (2003). I give my own account of habitual action in terms of goal-dependent automaticity in section 4, and extend it to the case of habitual virtuous action in section 5.

It seems correct to think that we want our virtuous actions to become effortless and habitual—a kind of second nature (McDowell 1995). We would like to act kindly or courageously without having to stop to think about whether and how kind or courageous action is needed. Yet, the very absence of deliberation and willful effort implied by the notion of habitual action falls foul of paradigms of rational thinking. I argue for the rationality of goal-dependent habitual virtuous actions in section 6. By the end of the chapter, I aim to have established that habitual virtuous actions can plausibly be explained by empirical psychology, that they can occur across objectively different situation-types, and that they are rational.

2. AUTOMATICITY

Dual process theory in cognitive and social psychology maintains that the mind's workings can be explained in terms of two basic kinds of cognitive processes: controlled and automatic. Here are the criteria for controlled processes: they are under the intentional control of the individual, and thus, present to awareness, flexible or subject to intervention, and effortful or constrained by the attentional resources available to the individual at the moment (Bargh 1989, 3–4). Here are the criteria for automatic processes: they are unintentional in the sense that they can occur even in the absence of explicit intentions or goals, involuntary, occurring outside of conscious awareness, autonomous or capable of running to completion without conscious intervention, not initiated by the conscious choice or will of the agent, and effortless in the sense that they will operate even when attentional resources are limited (Bargh 1989, 3, 5).[1] Deliberate or intentional action results from a controlled process; regularly performed actions that become habitual, such as typing or driving along a familiar route, are some examples of the workings of automatic processes.

A word or two of explanation about the criteria and my examples is in order. First, cognitive processes are now said by psychologists to satisfy "most or all" of the relevant classificatory criteria. Early in automaticity research, psychologists thought that a process must satisfy all of the relevant criteria to be considered as either controlled or automatic. As automaticity research extended from cognitive psychology to social psychology and processes of social cognition were studied, some researchers began to relax the standards for automaticity, acknowledging that a process could be considered automatic if it satisfied most, but not all, of the automaticity criteria, and controlled if it satisfied most, but not all, of the criteria for controlled cognitive processing (Devine and Monteith 1999, 343). Many actions seem to result from a complex mix of automatic and controlled processes.

Second, my examples might raise questions. Habitual typing and driving along a familiar route, for instance, seem puzzling as examples of automaticity, since they are action-sequences that do not satisfy all of the criteria. They are initiated by the conscious choice of the agent and are not beyond the agent's control. In what sense, then, would they be involuntary? In a moment, I will explain that there are different types of automaticity. Habitual typing and driving along a familiar route are examples of one type—goal-dependent automaticity—that is compatible with the voluntary initiation of an action sequence by an agent and with her ability to interrupt and control the sequence. That habitual typing and driving along a familiar route are now considered by psychologists to be examples of automatic actions illustrates how some automatic actions are said by psychologists to satisfy "most," but not all, of the criteria, and gives a hint of the inclusiveness of the category of automatic cognitive processes.

Another issue for philosophers might be that the categories carved out by the criteria are too rough. Velleman (2000, 4), for example, distinguishes three categories of phenomena: mere happenings, mere activities, and actions. Though the latter two are intentional, only actions exhibit full-blooded agency. According to Velleman (2000, 14), mere activities are "... those unforeseen movements to which a person is impelled by motives of which he is unaware," such as clumsily (yet adroitly) knocking over an ugly object on one's desk which one wants to replace, or a slip of the tongue that reveals one's true desires. Though mere activities are purposeful, one is not consciously aware of the intentions that motivate them. By contrast, full-blooded action, according to Velleman (2000, 14), is "... behavior whose first-order motives are perceived as reasons and are consequently reinforced by higher-order motives of rationality." Such actions, for Velleman, are autonomous and in the control of the agent, as opposed to mere activities that reveal an agent's intentions, yet happen without, or perhaps despite, the agent's conscious choice (see Velleman 2000, 6). As he puts it: "Mere activity is therefore a partial and imperfect exercise of the subject's capacity to make things happen: in one sense, the subject makes the activity happen; in another, it is made to happen despite him, or at least without his concurrence. Full-blooded human action occurs only when the subject's capacity to make things happen is exercised to its fullest extent" (2000, 4).

Could some habitual actions be mere activities, and not fully-blown, autonomous actions? As will become clear later, I believe that many habitual movements, such as typing and driving along a familiar route, satisfy Velleman's criteria for fully-blown, autonomous actions in the sense that the motives for such behavior are perceived as reasons that are, or would be, endorsed by the agent upon reflection, and the movements are in the agent's control in the sense that he or she initiates the action or action-sequence and can interrupt it at will. Yet such habitual actions, I argue, also satisfy most of the criteria for automaticity, such as being triggered by factors outside of the agent's conscious awareness, and being able to run to completion without the agent's conscious control.

Velleman's categories aside, we need to clarify the differences that psychologists have identified between controlled and automatic processes. Controlled processes are fairly familiar. If a cognitive process is controlled, it is intentional and present to conscious awareness. For example, if I decide to go to the refrigerator for a snack, the process of making that decision is intentional. I am aware that I want a snack. The action sequence of getting a snack is voluntary in the sense that I initiate it. The cognitive process of deciding to get a snack is flexible in the sense that I can intervene to direct, redirect, or interrupt the process. That is, I can change my mind about whether I want or need a snack, or decide to get some munchies from the cupboard instead of a yogurt from the refrigerator. All of this is effortful in the sense that it consumes attentional resources. I have to direct attention to the task of getting a snack—to whether and how I want to do this—and this places a demand on my processing capacity.

Automatic processes function differently. Several kinds of automatic processes have been identified, each with its own mechanism (Bargh 1989). Consider what has been called "preconscious automaticity" (Bargh 1989, 11–14). Stereotype activation provides a good example. Many of us have deeply held social stereotypes. Studies have shown that they can become activated and operative by triggering stimuli, such as skin color or gender characteristics, without our conscious awareness. But if my encountering a stimulus triggers a stereotype without my awareness, I do not intend that my subsequent action should be influenced by that stereotype, nor can I immediately deliberately intervene to control the effect the activated stereotype has on my action.[2] That is, the action, as influenced by the activated stereotype, is autonomous in the sense that it will run to completion without my being aware of, or exerting conscious control over, the stereotype's influence. Though I am aware that I am acting, I am not aware of the stereotype's influence on my action. Both the stereotype activation and the action as influenced by it are involuntary in the sense that I did not freely or deliberately choose for the stereotype to become activated, nor to act under its influence. Since the entire process of stereotype activation and influencing of action occurs outside of conscious awareness, it places no demands on my attentional resources. Thus, the process of stereotype activation and influencing of action satisfies all of the automaticity criteria: it is unintentional; occurring outside of conscious awareness; autonomous in the sense that, other things being equal, the activation and influencing of action runs to completion without conscious intervention or control; involuntary in the sense that it is not deliberately or freely chosen; and effortless in the sense that it does not tax attentional resources.

Preconscious automaticity is premised on the notion that mental representations can be activated via triggering events and can influence action without our awareness. John Bargh, a leading automaticity researcher, noted that goals are mentally represented, and hypothesized that goal-directed action can be produced by the repeated activation of the representation of a person's chronically held goal.[3] A chronically held goal is enduring or long-lived. A goal the mental representation of which is often activated by the appropriate stimuli becomes chronically accessible in the sense that it becomes readily activatable. In goal-dependent automaticity, goal activation occurs outside of the person's conscious awareness through encounters with triggering stimuli (Bargh et al. 2001, 1024; Chartrand and Bargh 1996, 465).

Initially, Bargh and his colleagues emphasized one main pathway through which environmental stimuli can activate representations of a person's chronic goals. In this route, the frequent and consistent pairing of situational features with goal-directed behaviors develops chronic situation-to-representation links (Chartrand and Bargh 1996, 465; Bargh and Gollwitzer 1994, 72; Bargh et al. 2001, 1015). Like other mental representations, goals and intentions are held in memory and can become activated by environmental stimuli. Representations of an individual's chronically held goals can repeatedly become activated in the same type of situation so that the mental association between situational features and goal-directed behavior becomes automatized. When an individual encounters the relevant situational features, the representation of the associated goal is directly but nonconsciously activated. The activated representation, in turn, sets in train plans to achieve the goal which flexibly unfold in interaction with changing information from the environment (Chartrand and Bargh 1996, 465; Bargh and Ferguson 2000, 932ff).

Automaticity researchers are clear that nonconsciously activated goal-directed behaviors are not reflex reactions to stimuli, but are intelligent, flexible responses to unfolding situational cues, and display many of the same qualities as consciously chosen actions (Bargh et al. 2001, 1014–1015; 1025). Bargh and his colleagues have identified the kinds of goals that are likely to be chronically held and the representations of which could be automatically activated (Bargh 1990, 111–119; Bargh and Gollwitzer 1994, 78–79). Among many types of enduring goals or commitments are those related to values, such as the goal of equity in social exchanges and the commitment to truth. These goals and commitments are likely to be expressed in different types of actions across many types of objectively different situations (Bargh 1990, 113–114; 118). Consider, for example, Cialdini's waiter (see Ross and Nisbett 1991, 164). Cialdini studied the highest-earning waiter in a restaurant over a period of time to find out what he did. The only consistent thing the waiter did was to pursue the goal of tip-maximization. His consistent pursuit of that goal led him to act differently with different types of customers. What made his behavior intelligible across objectively different situation-types was his consistent pursuit of his enduring goal.

Goals related to the pursuit of valued life tasks, such as parenting, and personal goals, such as being a high achiever or being a moral person, are also likely to be enduring and thus, their representations capable of being automatically activated (Bargh and Gollwitzer 1994, 79). Additional candidates for automatically activated goals are reactive goals, such as the disposition to be cooperative in interpersonal interactions (Bargh, 1990, 116–117). Social behaviors, such as cooperation and performing well, have been elicited through nonconscious goal activation (Bargh et al. 2001). Furthermore, when habits are established, the activation of the goal to act automatically elicits habitual behavior (Aars and Dijksterhuis 2000). Interestingly, recent studies indicate that temptations can activate overriding goal pursuits (Fishbach, Friedman, and Kruglanski 2003). These findings distinguish automatic goal activation from situational control, suggesting that automatic goal activation can counteract situational control and, like consciously chosen actions, promote the personal control of action in accordance with a person's values and priorities. For example, my encounter with a piece of delicious-looking chocolate cake can activate the representation of my goal to lose weight. An encounter with a situational cue triggers the representation of my chronically held goal, which can help me to resist temptation in the circumstances.

That value-relevant goals expressed across many objectively different types of situations, including interpersonal interactions, have been found to be enduring and thus, likely to become automatically activated, suggests that virtue-relevant goals can also be enduring and automatically activated across objectively different situation-types. If someone has an enduring virtue-relevant goal, such as being a just person, one's consistent goal pursuit could give rise to many different kinds of just actions as are appropriate for objectively different circumstances. If one repeatedly encounters circumstances that call for a just response, just actions could eventually be triggered by situational cues outside of one's conscious awareness. One's just actions could become habitual—the kinds of habitual actions that, over time, build up dispositions to just behavior.

In sum, nonconscious goal activation and automatic goal pursuit are well documented psychological phenomena. Higher level social behaviors such as cooperation and performing well, as well as habitual behaviors, have been shown to be produced through nonconscious goal activation. Moreover, psychologists have documented that some chronically held goals pertain to values, such as the goal of equity in social exchanges, being a good parent, and being a moral person. Given all of this, I believe that goal-dependent automaticity provides a promising framework for understanding habitual virtuous actions, through which virtuous dispositions can be formed.

3. POLLARD ON HABITUAL ACTIONS AND HABITUAL VIRTUOUS ACTIONS

To explain virtuous habits in terms of goal-dependent automaticity, we need an account of habitual virtuous action. For an account of habitual virtuous action, we need an account of habitual action. Pollard's (2003) account of habitual action is a good place to start. He wants to distinguish habits from reflexes, bodily processes, and compulsions (415). The centerpiece of his view is that habitual action has three features. It is repeated in the sense that "... the agent has a history of similar behaviours in similar contexts" (415). It is automatic in the sense that "... it does not involve the agent in deliberation about whether to act" (415). Finally, it is responsible, inasmuch as it is "... something the agent does, rather than something that merely happens to him" (415). The claim that habitual action is responsible action is key to the notion that habitual action is genuine action as opposed to mere behavior, that is, that agents are genuinely the authors of their habitual actions (Pollard 2003, 415).

According to Pollard, we are responsible for habitual actions because we have a certain kind of control over them. He calls this "intervention control," and distinguishes it from what he calls "direct control" (Pollard 2003, 415–416). We exert direct control when we deliberate about what to do, then do it. As I understand Pollard, direct control could also be called "initiation control," since it is the kind of control we exert when we initiate an action or action sequence. By contrast, intervention control occurs when we intervene in a behavior. The clearest example of intervention control, I believe, occurs when we stop ourselves while performing a familiar action sequence, and decide to redirect what we are doing, that is, to do it in a different way, or do something else entirely.

Pettit (2001, 38–39; 91–92) gives a nice account of habitual actions and of what is essentially intervention control. He notes that agents often act from habit, finding themselves in relatively familiar circumstances or exposed to familiar cues. The habitual actions they perform, he claims, are not actively caused by rationally held beliefs and desires, yet the actions conform, not by accident, to such beliefs and desires. Pettit (2001, 39) writes: "In such a case the rationally held beliefs and desires are not active causes that direct things this way or that, but standby causes that are ready to be activated in the event of things not going the way that they rationally require." The habitual actions are performed on "automatic pilot," yet, should unfamiliar prompts become apparent, the agent would be alerted to the fact that her actions were no longer satisfying her rationally held beliefs and desires, and would intervene, in accordance with conscious reflection, to redirect the action sequence. For example, suppose that I drive home from work each day along a familiar route. My driving this route has become habitual. I know where to turn, which lane to be in, and so on, and execute the required action sequence without much thinking. Suppose that one day, driving along with my attention elsewhere, I find myself passing the house on the corner at which I need to turn onto my street. The habitual action-sequence of my driving is interrupted. The unfamiliar cue of passing the house on the corner alerts me to the fact that I need to intervene to correct my routinized actions so as to satisfy my goal of getting home.

The possibility of intervention control enables us to be responsible for habitual actions, and thus, according to Pollard, distinguishes them from other repeated, automatic behaviors such as reflexes, bodily processes, and compulsions (Pollard 2003, 415–416). Though he admits the possibility of borderline cases (Pollard 2003, 416, n. 1), I remain skeptical that the possibility of intervention control alone clearly distinguishes habitual actions from reflexes, bodily processes, and compulsions. With time and practice, some reflexes and bodily processes can be brought under a fairly high degree of intervention control, if not direct control. For example, reflexes are important to athletes. Athletic training seeks to improve, through practice, reflex response time and coordination. Similarly, Buddhists use controlled breathing techniques as part of meditation practices. So it seems that at least some reflexes and bodily processes are not beyond the reach of some degree of intervention control.

Moreover, it seems that some of what Pollard considers to be repeated, automatic behaviors, such as cigarette smoking and fingernail biting, that fall under the heading of addictions or compulsions, are difficult, but not impossible, to control (Pollard 2003, 416, n. 1). Habitual cigarette smoking can be considered an addiction because cravings for nicotine and other chemicals in cigarettes are created by frequent smoking. Physical dependency on these drugs undermines smokers' capacities for intervention control. Yet even inveterate smokers are able to stub out a cigarette—to intervene to control their behavior. It is tempting to give a similar story for fingernail biting. Some nailbiters seem driven by a nervous need which appears close to a compulsion. Yet even nervous nailbiters can resist chewing their fingernails. In all of these cases, conscious effort or willfulness is needed to interrupt and redirect a reflex, a bodily process, or the addictive and compulsive behaviors of cigarette smoking and nailbiting. Intervention control can be successfully exerted. But if intervention control can be successfully exerted, we are responsible for these habits. Consequently, it seems that some instances of reflexes, bodily processes, and addictive and compulsive behaviors should not be excluded from the class of habitual actions, according to Pollard's three criteria. Based on these arguments, I am inclined to accept Pollard's three features as accurate descriptors of habitual actions, with the proviso, not pursued further here, that the criterion of intervention control needs to be supplemented to distinguish more clearly habitual actions from habitual behaviors.

Pollard (2003, 416) claims that all virtuous actions are habitual in the sense that they manifest his three features. Moreover, since no habitual actions are done for reasons in the accepted senses of internalism and externalism (Pollard 2003, 414), and all virtuous actions are habitual, it follows that no virtuous actions are done for reasons in the accepted senses. I think it is false both that all virtuous actions are habitual in Pollard's sense, and that no habitual action is done for a reason in an accepted sense. Consequently, I also think it is false that no virtuous actions are done for reasons in an accepted sense. To the contrary, as I will argue later, all virtuous actions, even automatic, habitual ones, are done for reasons in an accepted sense.

Consider first Pollard's argument that all virtuous actions are habitual (automatic) in the sense that no virtuous action requires deliberation about whether one should act. He considers but rejects the possibility that some virtuous actions result from deliberation. He imagines an objector claiming that deliberation is needed about when and how to act when one is acquiring a virtue, as well as when someone with an acquired virtue is faced with unfamiliar circumstances or an especially important decision (Pollard 2003, 416). Pollard admits that cases of virtue acquisition can require deliberation. Regarding deliberation from acquired virtue, he addresses the objection as follows:

> … it is characteristic of the virtuous agent that she will not think about *whether* to do what virtue requires (which would exclude the action from being automatic on my definition), but merely *how*. She thinks only about the details of the particular case. If she has to wonder about whether to do it, that only shows that she has not acquired the virtue, and that just means it has not yet become automatic in my sense. At other times, such as when an action is particularly urgent, or the circumstances are very familiar, she may not even deliberate about how to act, never mind whether. But even then, I do not think that should disqualify the action in question from being virtuous. Indeed deliberation in such circumstances would seem to detract from the virtue of the action, shading into an unhealthy obsession with deliberation, putting off the moment of action, rather than an appropriate practical response to a situation. Thus I think all virtuous actions are habitual. (416–417; italics in original)

Pollard's suggestion is that the person of acquired virtue need never deliberate about whether to act; if she does, this simply shows that she has not acquired the virtue. But surely this is false. Consider several cases. The first is a case in which a person of acquired virtue encounters a new situation. She is not sure whether she is required to act virtuously in the new situation. I would regard this not as a case of virtue acquisition, but of virtue extension—of extending or applying an acquired virtue in a new situation in which habitually performed virtuous action might be inapt. Perhaps a clearer case is one in which a person of acquired virtue must weigh virtuous action against virtuous inaction or non-intervention. A compassionate person might want to offer financial assistance to a recently unemployed friend, but refrain from doing so for fear of causing insult or wounding the other's pride. Whether to offer assistance is rightly the focus of deliberation, even for the person of acquired virtue. Another point merits mention. Pollard regards the need for deliberation about whether to act as evidence that virtue has not been fully acquired. But surely the need for deliberation about whether to act could in some cases be due to situational ambiguities and not to incompleteness in the acquisition of virtue. Deliberation about whether to act would focus on sorting out the ambiguities and discovering relevant facts to determine if action is truly required. So I think it is false that people of acquired virtue need not deliberate about whether to act. If so, some virtuous actions are done for reasons in an accepted sense. Consequently, not all virtuous actions are habitual in Pollard's sense.

I also think that there are situations in which people of acquired virtue need to deliberate about how to act—when they are in unfamiliar circumstances or facing matters of special urgency, for example. So I believe there are two broad categories of virtuous action: deliberative and habitual. The former includes cases of deliberation about whether and how to act. In cases of these kinds, virtuous people bring their practical wisdom to bear to act virtuously. Habitual virtuous actions proceed without the need for deliberation because practical wisdom has become automatic about certain things—certain deliberative routes have become canalized. Yet, the routinization of practical wisdom doesn't make it any the less practical wisdom.

Let us pause to glance back and look ahead. In the introduction to this chapter, I noted that the chapter focus is on explaining habitual virtuous actions—a means by which virtuous dispositions are built up over time—and in grounding these actions in empirical psychology. In section 2, I explained the difference between controlled and automatic cognitive processes, paying special attention to a particular kind of automatic process—goal-dependent automaticity. I argued that goal-dependent automaticity provides a promising framework for explaining habitual virtuous actions, as well as for explaining how such actions can exhibit a form of goal-oriented behavioral consistency across objectively different situation-types. In section 3, I examined and critiqued Pollard's (2003) account of habitual actions and of habitual virtuous actions. Sections 2 and 3 set the stage for section 4, in which I propose an alternative explanation to Pollard's account of habitual actions. There I advance my own account of generic habitual actions in terms of goal-dependent automaticity. In section 5, I extend my explanation of generic habitual actions to the case of habitual virtuous actions. There we will see why habitual virtuous actions need not be narrow behavioral regularities that are indexed to the objective features of situations, but can span objectively different situation-types. Finally, in section 6, I argue that habitual virtuous actions are rational.

4. EXPLAINING HABITUAL ACTIONS IN TERMS OF GOAL-DEPENDENT AUTOMATICITY

If we reflect on Pollard's three criteria for habitual actions, it becomes clear that they simply describe features of these actions without explaining why the actions have the characteristics they do. Goal-dependent automaticity provides an explanation for many habitual actions in the sense of giving an account of how and why we perform many of these actions and why they have distinctive features.

Consider criterion (1): habitual actions are repeated in the sense that the agent has a history of similar behaviors in similar contexts. This does not tell us why an agent performs similar behaviors in similar contexts. To get an explanation, we need not refer to the specific details of the agent's life. Many habitual actions are explained by (a) the agent's having a chronically accessible goal, and (b) the goal's being repeatedly activated by triggering environmental stimuli, resulting in (c) repeatedly occurring links between situational features and goal-directed behavior. Suppose that I drive home from work every day along the same route. It is likely that my driving home along this particular route is in the service of some chronically accessible goal, such as the goal of getting home in the most efficient way possible. The fact that my taking this route has become habitual means that traveling the route has features, such as minimal traffic and construction, that serve my goal. The specific actions that I take while driving the route, though responsive to environmental input such as changing traffic conditions, have become automatized. I find myself driving without the need for highly focused attention or deliberation, for example, about when and where I should turn.

Pollard's second criterion is (2): habitual actions do not involve the agent in deliberations about whether to act. Consider again my habitual action of driving home from work every day along the same route. Since my actions have become routinized, I do not deliberate about whether to drive the familiar route, nor, while on the route, need I deliberate about when and where to turn, which lane to be in, and so on. Two points about my state of conscious awareness are apt. First, we might intuitively describe the mental state I am in by saying that I am on "automatic pilot." Automaticity researchers would say that my frequently repeated actions have become so routinized that my attentional resources are not fully engaged by what I am doing. This frees my cognitive capacities for other tasks, such as having a conversation with my passengers or thinking over the day's events. Though I am not in a "twilight" state of conscious awareness, as occurs when one is falling asleep or waking up, nor in a daze, I am not fully paying attention to my driving. However, I am aware of, and responsive to, environmental stimuli. The phenomenological feel of the automatic pilot mental state in which attentional resources are not concentrated on the task at hand can be highlighted by contrasting the familiar experience of driving along a well-traveled route in good weather with the kind of highly focused attention and awareness needed either to drive the same route under very bad weather conditions, such as during a severe snowstorm, or when driving along an unfamiliar road at night. There is a considerable difference in the level and intensity of the attentional resources needed to perform each kind of task. Second, though I am consciously aware that I am driving, I may be unaware that my driving is in the service of a goal, and inattentive to the fact that my specific actions, such as stopping, turning, slowing down, and so on, are in response to triggering situational features. My familiar, routinized actions will run autonomously to completion unless unexpected events require me to intervene.

Pollard's third criterion is (3): habitual actions are responsible in the sense that they are under the agent's intervention control. I can intervene to stop or redirect the action sequence, but doing so requires effort and attention. I can take myself off of automatic pilot and go "online" with my cognitive and attentional resources. This simply means that I have switched to another mode of cognitive processing: an intervention signals the fact that I have left the automatic mode of cognitive processing and entered the controlled mode.

Two points should be made about the foregoing account. First, as I will argue more fully in section 6, goal-directed automatic actions are done for a reason. The reason that these automatic, habitual actions are performed is to serve the agent's chronically accessible goals. Thus, habitual, automatized goal-dependent actions are purposive. The agent's reason for acting—to serve a chronic goal—is not present to her consciousness at the time of acting, but is operative in her psychological economy, and is such that, were it brought to her conscious awareness, she would endorse it as her reason for acting. Her reason for acting is a motivating factor that both explains her actions and justifies or would justify them, should the agent reflect upon them.

Second, some habitual actions might not be obviously explicable in terms of chronically accessible goals. There could be patterns of habitual actions that we do without being motivated, consciously or otherwise, to attain a goal. So I do not want to claim that all habitual actions result from goal-dependent automaticity. We might use the categories of Velleman (2000) and contend that habitual actions that do not serve an agent's goals are not genuine actions, but mere activities. However one resolves the question of how to categorize habitual actions that do not serve an agent's goals, it is plausible to think that for many habitual actions, there is a goal that is independently intelligible, that is, not simply consequentially ascribable to the agent in virtue of her performance of habitual actions, the attribution of which explains the actions or aspects of the actions.[4] That is, some goals are sufficiently content-rich to explain habitual actions that would remain opaque or puzzling unless the goal is ascribed to the agent. Consider the example of driving home every day along the same route. If someone were to ask me or if I were to ask myself why I habitually take the same route, it would be informative to answer that I have the goal of getting home in the most efficient way possible. Ascribing that goal would explain that I value efficiency in travel over other desiderata, such as having a pleasant view en route, and that I believe that efficiency is obtained through advantages that my habitual route offers, such as minimal construction and traffic. Even though the goal is not present to my conscious awareness at the time of acting, it can be elicited and endorsed through reflection on why I act as I do.

Let us take stock. Goal-dependent automaticity allows us to explain three features of habitual action:

1. Habitual actions are repeated in the sense that the agent has a history of similar behaviors in similar contexts.
2. Habitual actions are automatic in the sense that they do not involve the agent in deliberations about whether to act.
3. Habitual actions are responsible in the sense that they are under the agent's intervention control.

And to add:

4. Some habitual actions are goal-dependent in the sense that they serve an agent's chronically accessible goals.

A corollary of (4), discussed more fully in section 6, is:

5. Goal-dependent habitual actions are purposive and rational; that is, the fact that habitual actions serve an agent's goals explains how those actions can be rational.

5. EXPLAINING HABITUAL VIRTUOUS ACTIONS IN TERMS OF GOAL-DEPENDENT AUTOMATICITY

With this framework in hand, we can explain habitual virtuous actions in terms of goal-dependent automaticity. The basic framework of the explanation is the same as that given above. Habitual virtuous actions are explained by saying that: (a) the agent has a chronically accessible mental representation of a virtue-relevant goal, (b) her mental representation of the goal is repeatedly but nonconsciously activated by triggering environmental stimuli, and repeated nonconscious activation of the represented goal results in (c) repeated links between situational features and goal-directed behavior. In this way, virtuous actions become automatic and routinized.

Aspects of the explanation need further development. Let us make clear at the outset that explaining the acquisition or origin of habitual virtuous actions is not part of the account. Virtuous habits can be acquired in many ways, for example, unintentionally, through upbringing, or through the natural human capacity to do the same actions, as well as through having a virtue-relevant goal. However, for a mature agent to be considered truly virtuous, virtuous actions must be performed for the right reasons, that is, with the appropriate motivation. The account of habitual virtuous actions in terms of goal-dependent automaticity is meant to explain the acquired virtuous habits of the mature agent.

To develop the account, let us begin with what it means to say that an agent has a chronically accessible mental representation of a virtue-relevant goal. We need to explain what is meant by the phrase, "virtue-relevant goal," and what it means for the representation of a goal to be chronically accessible. Let us start with the notion of a virtue-relevant goal.

The notion of a virtue-relevant goal can be made clearer, I believe, by referring to the idea of a value-relevant goal. Examples of value-relevant goals were given in section 2 and include the goal of equity in social exchanges and the commitment to truth. A value-relevant goal is a goal which, if the agent had it, would, under the appropriate conditions, result in the agent's performing value-expressive actions, that is, actions that express a commitment to the value in question. Similarly, I propose to define virtue-relevant goal as follows: A virtue-relevant goal is a goal which, if the agent had it, would, under the appropriate conditions, result in the agent's performing virtue-expressive, that is, virtuous, actions. Deliberative as well as non-deliberative, habitual virtuous actions can result from an agent's having a virtue-relevant goal. Appropriate conditions include environmental stimuli that activate the represented goal, and the absence or failure of action-inhibiting factors.

If we accept the definition of virtue-relevant goal, it follows that an agent need not have the goal of being virtuous *tout court*, or even the goal of being virtuous in the sense of having a goal to have a specific virtue, such as patience or courage, to have goals which would result in her performing virtuous actions. An agent might have the goal of being a good parent, good colleague, good nurse, good citizen, or good friend. Having these goals would result in the agent's performing virtuous actions, since these roles carry associated virtues. The goals of helping others, promoting peace, or being a fair or decent person are also virtue-relevant in the sense that having them would result in an agent's performing virtuous actions.

So far, however, the account seems to suffer from circularity: an action is virtuous just in case it expresses virtuous motivation. To avoid the circle, we need to distinguish between virtuous actions, which only express virtuous motivations, and truly or genuinely virtuous actions, which both express virtuous motivations and successfully hit the target of virtue because they incorporate practical wisdom. Truly virtuous actions hit the target of virtue because they result from deliberative excellence or practical wisdom, and not through accident or happenstance. As noted earlier, deliberative excellence can become canalized in genuinely virtuous actions that are habitual, and is no less practical wisdom for having become habitual.

Is the attribution of a virtue-relevant goal necessary to explain someone's habitual virtuous actions? Someone might argue that it is not. Suppose that Tim has a history of performing habitually just actions.[5] We can infer from the facts of Tim's life that he is habitually just. Need we go further than this and say that, in addition, he has the goal of being just? What does positing a goal add? If positing a goal would add no information in explaining Tim's habitual actions being virtuous beyond what can be gotten from inference from his actions alone, then having a virtue-relevant goal is not necessary for habitual virtuous actions.

In response, I would say that we need more information than that gleaned from knowledge of Tim's habitual actions alone before we can reliably infer that Tim is truly virtuous. We need to know about the nature of Tim's motivations. Suppose that Tim appears to be habitually just because he wants to be like his father, who is a genuinely just man. Tim does not have the goal of being just or of being fair-minded, but has the goal of being like his father. If his father were unjust, Tim would be unjust. Tim's having the goal of being like his father seems to result in his performing habitual virtuous actions. Yet I would not want to claim that Tim is genuinely just, on the grounds that his putatively just actions are done for the wrong reasons. It should be noted that Tim's motivations could be quite fragmented—perhaps a different psychological structure leads to his habitually just actions on different occasions. In this case, too, an inference from Tim's habitual actions to a virtuous disposition would be mistaken. There would be no coherent psychological structure that could be identified as a "virtue" in the traditional sense.

The example of Tim illustrates the possibility of mistakenly inferring a genuinely virtue-relevant goal from patterns of habitual actions alone, without sufficient attention to the agent's motivations for acting. If we infer from Tim's habitual actions that he is truly virtuous, we mistakenly attribute virtuous motivations to him when in fact he lacks them. The possibility of being mistaken shows that virtue cannot reliably be inferred solely from habitual actions. To fully explain the truly virtuous nature of an agent's habitual actions, we need to refer to his virtue-relevant goals, which provide us with information about his motives. Lacking virtue-relevant goals, an agent will lack the motivations needed to be genuinely virtuous. Consequently, having a virtue-relevant goal is necessary for an agent to perform habitual virtuous actions and is an essential part of explanations of habitual actions that are truly virtuous.

Is this a question-begging response? I think not. According to virtue ethicists, truly virtuous action must be performed for the right reasons or motives.[6] A range of motivations, such as wanting to be a good parent, or having the goal of helping others, qualify as appropriate. Other motivations, such as having the goal of being like one's father, or performing charity work simply to look good, indicate that true virtue has not been attained. In other words, virtue is not simply a matter of acting or even of acting habitually, but also of having fine inner states or dispositions that ground one's actions. This traditional view of the nature of virtue—that it depends on an agent's motivations as well as on her actions—has been advanced independently of the automaticity account of habitual virtuous actions, which posits that chronically accessible virtue-relevant goals, activated outside of the agent's conscious awareness, are necessary for habitual virtuous actions. In explaining the psychology of habitual virtuous action, the automaticity account begs no questions by drawing on the independently accepted idea that virtuous action requires appropriate motivation.

What are we to say about changes in goals? Suppose that for many years, I have the goal of being patient. Repeated activations of my goal under the appropriate conditions result in my developing habits of patient actions. I then abandon my goal, but, through the "force of habit," that is, through the natural human tendency to continue doing the same thing, I continue performing patient actions. The actions can no longer be explained by reference to a virtue-relevant goal, however, since I have abandoned it.

We might use Velleman's (2000) categories to say that the habitual actions that I perform after I abandon my goal of being patient are not genuine human actions, but are mere activities. I admitted in section 4 that some habitual actions are not explicable by reference to an agent's chronically accessible goals and, consequently, can be thought of as mere activities. We simply do such activities without being motivated to attain a goal. However we regard these activities—as mere activities or as actions in some fuller sense —they no longer qualify as virtuous, since they are done from force of habit alone and not from motivations that can count as virtuous. Truly virtuous actions, including truly virtuous habitual actions, are actions done with practical wisdom for the right reasons, not for the wrong reasons or for no reasons.

So far we have been explaining the meaning of virtue-relevant goal and why having a virtue-relevant goal is necessary for an agent to perform habitual virtuous actions. What does it mean to say that a represented goal is chronically accessible? In the context of goal-dependent automaticity, a chronically accessible goal should be understood as having two dimensions or aspects: temporal duration and accessibility. First, if an agent has a chronically held goal, she has a mental representation of that goal that is part of her knowledge base. The representation is temporally enduring or long-lived. Second, a chronically accessible goal is a goal the mental representation of which is readily activated by the appropriate stimuli. If automaticity researchers are correct, a mental representation which is activated need not be present to conscious awareness. That is, certain thoughts may be active without our being aware of them. Though this might seem mysterious, it is actually a familiar part of our everyday experience. Struggling with a recalcitrant argument, I put the work aside and take the evening off. The next morning, the argument is clearer and I can see my way through. A likely explanation of the phenomenon is that thoughts pertaining to the argument, though not present to my conscious awareness, were nonetheless active in my mind.

How are we to understand mental representations of goals? If a person has a representation of the goal of being just, she has some idea of what justice requires, and of what injustice amounts to. To be more precise, she probably has a very complex idea of justice and injustice based on reading she has done and real-life episodes she has encountered. These ideas by themselves do not comprise the entire representation of her goal. In addition, the representation must include some representation of her own role vis-à-vis justice and injustice. Otherwise, it would not be *her* goal that is being represented, but a complex of impersonal ideas about justice and injustice. The representations of goals that are activated to produce habitual actions are representations of *my* aims, such as my aim of being a good parent, that is, what being a good parent means to me in my life, and not of abstract, impersonal goals that anyone might have.

Mental representations of goals, of course, need to be activated if actions are to result. We are not justified in ascribing chronically accessible goals to agents independently of facts about their actions.

So far our explanation of habitual virtuous actions has focused on what it means for an agent to have a chronically accessible mental representation of a virtue-relevant goal. The next part of the explanation posits that the mental representation of the goal is repeatedly but nonconsciously activated by encounters with triggering environmental stimuli, and that repeated activation eventually forms situation-behavior links. Through repetition, a three-way connection is forged between activated goal representation, situational triggers, and goal-directed behavior. Thus, with repetition, virtuous actions become habitual—performed automatically, without conscious deliberation on the part of the agent.

On the face of it, this explanation might sound implausible. Nonconscious goal activation is the sticking point. One might accept every part of the explanation, but balk at the claim that repeated activation of the represented goal occurs outside of conscious awareness. For truly virtuous actions to result, it is intuitively more plausible to think that the entire process must be present to conscious awareness; that is, that the agent must be aware of perceiving relevant situational cues and of having her goal activated. Seeing a child bullied on the playground, or an elderly woman being cheated by a sales clerk should be very salient to the virtuous person's consciousness—it should make her blood boil.

Two points should be made in response. First, for the agent to act truly virtuously, it is not necessary that she be consciously aware that the representation of her virtue-relevant goal has been activated. Second, it is not necessary that she be aware of all of the situational cues to which she responds.

The second point is easier to see than the first. In the case of the child being bullied on a playground or the elderly woman being cheated, it is evident that some situational cues are consciously perceived by the virtuous agent. The just person sees the child being bullied; she is witness to the elderly woman's plight. Admitting these obvious facts about what the virtuous person must perceive to be motivated to act is compatible with the likelihood that other, more subtle cues are perceived but not consciously registered by the agent. Perhaps something about the bullied child or the elderly woman is picked up on by the virtuous person, and she responds to these features of the one in need. After the fact, the virtuous person might not be able to explain what it was about the situation that elicited her response. Yet, a measure of the depth and nuance of a person's virtue is her ability to effortlessly or intuitively pick up on and respond to subtle cues that someone of less developed virtue might miss.

But, if the virtuous person is unaware that she is responding to subtle situational cues, she could also be unaware that the situation has activated a virtue-relevant goal. Of course, there probably are cases in which someone knows a virtue-relevant goal has been activated by a situation. But even in obvious cases, such as that of the child being bullied or the woman being cheated, an agent need not be aware that her goal has been activated and is influencing her actions. She might think to herself, for example, "I saw what was happening to that woman, and it made my blood boil. I just had to do something." Only later, upon analyzing the situation, might she realize that her sense of justice was engaged. Her realization that she acted to prevent injustice need not have been present to her conscious awareness at the time of acting. In other words, realizing that one is acting virtuously at the time of acting is not a necessary condition for genuinely virtuous action.

The fact that some virtuous actions are nonconsciously activated and habitually executed largely outside of conscious awareness explains why they are performed effortlessly, apparently without the need for concentration of attention or overt deliberation. It also explains why it is plausible to think that the virtuous person would be unable to give a complete account of the perceptions, cognitions, and motivations that produce her own virtuous actions or to explain to others exactly when and how they ought to act virtuously (Johnson 2003, 827–828). Moral advice accounts are said to flounder because the nuances of virtuous action are difficult, if not impossible, to articulate and explain. The reason is that the virtuous person lacks full information, not only about the character and circumstances of others, but also about her own habitual perceptions and responses. Suppose that I characteristically show courage in just the right way at just the right moment, then am called upon later to explain how and why I did what I did. It is notoriously difficult to put into words, both at the time of acting and *ex post facto,* my thoughts and motivations for my actions. Automaticity explains at least a part of this difficulty. Our goals are nonconsciously activated by situational features; our action sequences flexibly and intelligently unfold on a moment by moment basis in interaction with information received from the environment without our need to consciously register all cues and responses. The cognitive and motivational processes that direct our habitual actions, which need not be irrational, operate largely outside of conscious awareness and thus, are often not immediately accessible to us either at the time of acting or upon subsequent reflection.

In the history of psychology, the unconscious has been viewed as the repository of deeply held goals and motives (Ellenberger 1970; Bargh and Barndollar 1996). Why not think that deeply held moral commitments, such as the goal of being virtuous or of being a good parent or colleague, also reside in the unconscious, and are called into action by situational cues operating outside of conscious awareness? Why think that goals of these types function only at the surface level of conscious deliberation, and do not more deeply permeate our thoughts and actions? An analogy with native language speakers is apt. Just as native language speakers effortlessly and correctly use complex rules of grammar and syntax without conscious deliberation or being able to explain how or why they use them, so, too, we can initiate and execute many complex social actions, including habitual virtuous actions, without needing to deliberate or being able to explain how or why. Our abilities to speak and act are due to the operation, in interaction with environmental cues, of deep-seated cognitive and linguistic structures. Similarly, the automaticity account of habitual virtuous action is a depth account of virtuous practice, explaining in terms of deep-seated cognitive and motivational processes how and why it is that virtue can go all the way down or become second nature (Hursthourse 1999; McDowell 1995).[7] Automaticity neither challenges nor replaces, but instead, supplements accounts of truly virtuous actions in terms of conscious or surface-level deliberation and choice.

6. THE RATIONALITY OF HABITUAL VIRTUOUS ACTIONS

Earlier I claimed that habitual virtuous actions are rational because they serve the agent's goals. Their goal-dependency renders them purposive and gives them a rational grounding. Saying this does not get us very far, however. More explanation is needed.

According to the automaticity account, an agent's having a chronically accessible mental representation of a virtue-relevant goal is a necessary, but not sufficient condition of her performing habitual virtuous actions. Virtue-relevant goals are easily analyzable in terms of an agent's beliefs and desires—beliefs about what virtue requires generally and in specific situations, and desires or commitments to following through with virtuous actions. Thus, goal-dependent habits are essentially linked with an agent's mental states. An agent's virtue-relevant goals provide the motivating reasons for her performance of habitual virtuous actions.

Moreover, goal-dependent automaticity demystifies the sense in which an agent's reasons for acting need not be present to her conscious awareness at the time of acting, yet are "... in some sense, 'present' to the agent" (Pollard 2003, 414). Her reasons for acting are nonconscious elements of her psyche operating outside of conscious awareness at the time of acting. The operation of nonconscious cognitive and motivational factors on action is neither unfamiliar nor mysterious. Nonconscious desires, such as the desires to please someone, to cooperate, or to perform well, can operate outside of conscious awareness to influence our performance on tasks (see Bargh 1990; Bargh et al. 2001; Fitzsimons and Bargh 2003; Shah 2003; and Fitzsimons et al. 2005). Furthermore, knowledge, such as knowledge of rules regulating the movements of chess pieces or grammatical rules covering verb conjugations or subject-predicate agreement, is nonconsciously functioning as we play chess, speak, or write. Similarly, virtue-relevant goals nonconsciously motivate, partially explain, and can justify habitual virtuous actions.

Pollard (2003, 424) offers a different account of how habitual virtuous actions can be considered rational while not requiring that the content of the reasons be present to the agent's consciousness at the time of acting. According to him, the justification or rationalization of an agent's habitual actions depends on the creative construction of an account of how those actions in their immediate context cohere with her overall world-view, projects, motivations, and so on. In other words, habitual actions can be justified by constructing a narrative, or telling a story, about how those actions fit within the agent's life and overall world-view.

However, as Pollard would no doubt agree, to be more than a coherent fiction, the narrative must have contact with reality. Pollard might also agree that the agent should sometimes be able to construct the narrative. I propose that contact with the agent's reality should be grounded in the notion that her habitual virtuous actions link ultimately, though nonconsciously at the time of acting, with her virtue-relevant goals. In principle, then, the kind of justification we are after has a narrative aspect in the sense that we can tell a coherent story justifying the agent's habitual virtuous actions from a third person perspective. But this story should also be available to the agent from her first person perspective. Reflecting on the virtuous habits she has acquired, she should be able to honestly and intelligibly link them with her own virtue-relevant goals. In other words, the agent herself should be able to reflectively endorse the justificatory narrative, even though she is not conscious of the content of her reasons for acting when she acts. She can reflectively endorse this kind of justificatory narrative because virtue-relevant goals are items in her psychological make-up which link, through repeated activation with triggering features, conceptually and practically with her habitual virtuous actions.

Is the notion of reflective endorsement of a justificatory narrative in tension with the depth account of virtue-relevant goals and with the difficulty, noted earlier, of articulating the perceptions and motivations that accompany virtuous action? There is tension, but it is not serious. Nothing in the depth account precludes the possibility that, through reflection, deep-seated goals can be brought to conscious awareness. To be sure, the justificatory narrative can vary in its sweep and complexity. The story could be as simple as an agent's telling herself that she had to tell an unpleasant truth on a specific occasion because she is just "not the sort of person who lies," or that she corrected a cashier's mistake in her favor because she is essentially honest in her dealings. The important point is that the agent can regard her virtuous actions as justified because she does or would recognize them as serving virtue-relevant goals that she does or would endorse upon reflection.

7. CONCLUSION

Let us pause to take stock. The aim of this volume is to provide an empirically grounded theory of virtue. The project was begun in chapter 1, where I advanced an empirically supported conception of traits—CAPS traits—and claimed that a subset of these traits can plausibly be considered virtues. Empirical evidence has shown that these traits produce behavior that is consistent across objectively different situation-types. This is because CAPS traits are keyed to the meanings that situations have for people. The importance of this feature, I believe, has not been sufficiently appreciated by situationist philosophers. If virtues are a subset of CAPS traits, situationist worries about the empirical inadequacy of many versions of virtue ethics are laid to rest. In chapter 1, I also drew on studies in the psychology of prejudice to sketch how CAPS traits, though they might initially be local, can be generalized across objectively different situation-types to approximate globality in some personalities.

Our story did not end there, however. Chapter 1 assumes that we begin with traits, whether local or more extensive, then undertake from there the task of deliberate virtue cultivation and vice inhibition. In this chapter, I've amplified the account by arguing that another way in which virtuous dispositions are formed—through habitual virtuous actions—can also be plausibly explained by empirical psychology. Goal-dependent automaticity provides an empirically adequate psychological framework for understanding habitual virtuous actions. According to this framework, repeated encounters with situational cues trigger an agent's virtue-relevant goals outside of her conscious awareness, resulting in her habitual performance of virtuous actions in those circumstances. Because virtue-relevant goals can be activated in many objectively different situation-types, habitual virtuous actions need not be narrowly confined behavioral regularities, but are flexible and intelligent actions that can cross objectively different types of situations. Truly virtuous habitual actions, it should be noted, not only express virtuous motivations, but incorporate practical wisdom, which can become routinized, thereby allowing agents to regularly hit the targets of virtuous action. Virtue-relevant goals not only provide motivating reasons for habitual virtuous actions, but can justify those actions by their incorporation into a justificatory narrative that the agent does or would reflectively endorse.

This is not yet the end of the story. Many versions of virtue ethics hold that virtue helps us to live well. How and why does virtue do this? I answer this question by invoking another research topic in empirical psychology—work on social intelligence. I contend that virtue helps in social living because it is a form of social intelligence. What social intelligence is and why it matters are the topics of chapter 3. In chapter 4, I argue that virtue is a form of social intelligence. Understanding social intelligence and recognizing that virtue is a form of it, I believe, helps to explain in large part how and why virtue enables us to live well.

3

SOCIAL INTELLIGENCE AND WHY IT MATTERS

1. INTRODUCTION

In chapters one and two, I've developed the main features of an empirically adequate theory of virtue. I've contended that virtues are CAPS traits—traits that are manifested in consistent behavior across objectively different situation types. In addition, I've maintained that virtues can be cultivated by the deliberate efforts of agents to shape their characters, or through habitual virtuous actions that can be explained in terms of goal-dependent automaticity. In the next two chapters, I extend this account by offering an empirically supported explanation of how and why virtue makes our lives go better. According to classical eudaimonism, virtue enables us to live well because it enables us to achieve goals which are necessary for flourishing. Virtues help us to achieve these goals, I contend, because they are forms of social intelligence. In this chapter, I explain what social intelligence is and make a case for its empirical adequacy. In the next, I argue that virtues are forms of social intelligence.

Social intelligence, as studied by psychologists, can be loosely defined as the knowledge, cognitive abilities, and affective sensitivities, such as empathy, that enable us to navigate our social world.[1] More colloquially, we can describe social intelligence as "people smarts," and contrast it with academic intelligence, or "book smarts." Social intelligence is that aspect of our personalities that enables us to perceive and respond to the interpersonal dynamics of situations. Since virtue is concerned with our abilities to perceive and respond to interpersonal situations, it would seem that the notion of social intelligence is of interest to virtue theory.

An array of definitions, theories, and empirical research from intelligence theory and personality theory in psychology suggests that social intelligence is remarkably complex. Is the empirical research on social intelligence sufficiently robust to make the study of social intelligence worthwhile to virtue theorists? The question of the empirical adequacy of social intelligence research is taken up in section 2 of this chapter. There I contend that social intelligence research passes empirical muster in its own right. I also argue that it meshes well with the cognitive-affective, goal-oriented conception of personality favored by the psychological research traditions already appealed to in this book—the social-cognitivist approach of Mischel and Shoda, the automaticity theories of Bargh and others, as well as with the emphasis of social psychologists Ross and Nisbett (1991) on cognitive-affective construal. Thus, the study of social intelligence is at home in the study of personality, and understanding social intelligence is integral to understanding personality and its functioning.

In section 3, I sketch a theory of social intelligence. What would such a theory entail? A theory of social intelligence, I believe, would explain both the cognitive-affective processes that constitute social intelligence and how social intelligence operates in our lives. I draw mainly on the work of personality theorists Cantor and Kihlstrom (1987) to explain both the processes that comprise social intelligence and its functions. In sections 4 and 5, I explore the notion of social intelligence in more detail by contrasting it with related concepts. I address in section 4 the notions of social intelligence, social competence, and social incompetence, and in section 5, I distinguish social intelligence from wisdom.

2. THE EMPIRICAL ADEQUACY OF SOCIAL INTELLIGENCE RESEARCH

Psychologists have suggested several definitions of social intelligence. An early account by E. L. Thorndike (1920) divides intelligence into three facets. According to Thorndike, abstract intelligence is the ability to understand and manage ideas; mechanical intelligence, the ability to understand and manage concrete objects; and social intelligence, the ability to understand and manage people— "… to act wisely in human relations" (Thorndike, quoted in Kihlstrom and Cantor 2000, 359). Like Thorndike, other early theorists also think of social intelligence as facility in getting along with people (Moss and Hunt 1927; Hunt 1928), or construe social intelligence as sensitivity to social stimuli and cues, and insight into others' moods, temperaments, and personalities (Strang 1930; Vernon 1933; Wedeck 1947; Wechsler 1958). More recently, social intelligence has been defined as "… the individual's fund of knowledge about the social world" (Kihlstrom and Cantor 2000, 359). According to Greenspan and Love (1997, 311), social intelligence "... refers to one's ability to understand interpersonal situations and transactions and to use that understanding to assist one in achieving desired interpersonal outcomes ... social intelligence may be considered the cognitive underpinning of social competence and is an important contributor to success in social activities such as work and personal relationships." Common to these definitions is the idea that social intelligence is the knowledge or understanding needed to perform well in social life.

Social intelligence is not purely cognitive, however. Goleman (2006, 1–12) adopts Thorndike's view that social intelligence is the ability to act wisely in human relationships. He further divides social intelligence into social awareness and social facility (Goleman 2006, 84). Among the components comprising social awareness is empathy, or feeling with others and sensing non-verbal affective cues (Goleman 2006, 84). Among the components of social facility is concern, which Goleman (2006, 84) describes as "[c]aring about others' needs and acting accordingly."

Three different empirical approaches have been used to study social intelligence. We can call them the psychometric, idiographic, and "implicit theory" approaches. Consider first the psychometric method of studying social intelligence. As the name psychometric implies, proponents believe that the psychological attributes of persons can be identified, measured, and compared. At home in the study of intelligence and learning, this method views social intelligence as a configuration of traits and abilities that people possess. Proponents of the psychometric approach maintain that individual performances on social intelligence-related tasks, such as judgment in social situations and recognizing the mental state of a speaker, can be measured, rated, and compared.

The second empirical approach is idiographic. Exemplified by the work of personality theorists Cantor and Kihlstrom (1987) and by Taylor (1990), this approach does not focus on measuring the individual's social intelligence relative to some norm or standard, but seeks to understand the cognitive structures and processes out of which personality is constructed and how they operate in people's lives (Kihlstrom and Cantor 2000, 368, 371).

The third approach to the empirical study of social intelligence has been characterized as an "implicit theoretical approach" (Kihlstrom and Cantor 2000, 367; Sternberg and Smith 1985, 169–170). Its method is to discover what laypeople mean by social intelligence by investigating their implicit or tacit understandings of the concept.[2] Though interesting, the implicit theoretical approach is not relevant to my project, and so, will be left aside.

How do the psychometric and idiographic approaches to the study of social intelligence relate to each other? One way of explaining how they relate is by viewing them as complementary. On this view, we start with a conception of social intelligence derived from the study of individual lives. This conception identifies the cognitive and affective processes involved in social intelligence, explains how it is acquired, how it changes, and how it functions. The psychometric approach then tests the extent to which people possess the various factors which constitute social intelligence as defined by the idiographic approach. If the analysis of the idiographic approach is correct, we should expect that social intelligence differs from academic intelligence, and psychometrics confirms this.

The major breakthrough in the psychometric approach to social intelligence research occurred with Ford and Tisak (1983).[3] Until then, researchers had little success in detecting an empirically coherent domain for social intelligence that was separate from academic intelligence. Ford and Tisak credit their success in establishing the separateness of social from academic intelligence to their use of a behavioral effectiveness definition of social intelligence tested by multiple measures. In a study involving over six hundred high school students, they used four measures of mathematical and verbal ability derived from grade reports and standardized test scores to gauge the academic intelligence of subjects, then tested social intelligence by means of self, peer, and teacher ratings of social competence, an empathy test, self-reports of social competence, and an interview rating. The researchers found evidence for the separability of academic intelligence and behavioral effectiveness.

Similar findings have been obtained by other investigators who administered personality measures tapping aspects of social intelligence.[4] For example, Lee, Wong, Day, Maxwell, and Thorpe (2000) confirmed and extended previous analyses of social and academic intelligence. In a study using 169 college students, they confirmed the multidimensionality of social and academic intelligence—each consists of conceptual or propositional knowledge and problem-solving abilities—and extended previous research with evidence that academic and social intelligences are relatively distinct domains. In a study of 239 undergraduates, Lee, Day, Meara, and Maxwell (2002) replicated prior findings that social intelligence consists of social knowledge as well as problem-solving ability, and found evidence suggesting that social knowledge, social problem-solving ability, and creativity could involve similar or overlapping mental processes. Using performance measures that tested 118 high school and first-year college students, Weis and Suss (2007) provided empirical evidence for the multidimensionality of social intelligence as consisting of social knowledge, social understanding or interpretative ability, and social memory.

Since the foregoing experiments confirm and replicate prior results, I believe they pass empirical muster in their own right. They chart a realm of intelligent behavior specific to social interactions and separate from other forms of intelligence. How well does this research mesh with other research on personality that is of interest to virtue theory? My view is that social intelligence research from both the idiographic and the psychometric perspectives nicely complements the cognitive-affective, goal-oriented conception of personality favored by Mischel and Shoda, social psychologists Ross and Nisbett, and Bargh and other automaticity researchers.

Consider Mischel and Shoda's CAPS theory of personality. To move beyond the situationist impasse in personality theory, Mischel and his collaborators focused on the importance of the subjective meanings that situations have for people. That is, they concentrated on how people interpret or construe situations to find evidence of behavioral consistency and personality coherence. Social intelligence research investigates the mechanisms of construal used in interpersonal situations—the knowledge, interpretative skills, memories, problem-solving abilities, and affective sensitivities needed to function well in the social domain. Consequently, social intelligence research meshes well with the CAPS approach to personality by extending our knowledge of the mechanisms of construal theorized as essential to personality functioning by CAPS.

Social psychologists Ross and Nisbett (1991, 8–17) write of a conceptual "tripod" on which social psychology rests: situations, construal, and the concept of a tension system. The last two legs of the tripod have to do with cognitive-affective construal. Regarding the principle of construal, they write:

> The second enduring contribution of social psychology, ironically, is one that challenges the theoretical and practical value of the doctrine of situationism. The impact of any "objective" stimulus situation depends upon the personal and subjective meaning that the actor attaches to that situation. To predict the behavior of a given person successfully, we must be able to appreciate the actor's construal of the situation—that is, the manner in which the person understands the situation as a whole. Construal issues are similarly important if our goal is to control or change behavior. (11)

The third leg of the tripod on which social psychology rests is the concept of a tension system (Ross and Nisbett 1991, 13–17). This is the idea that individual psyches and behavior exist in a field of dynamic forces. In other words, to understand behavior, we need to understand the totality of forces operative in the field within which behavior occurs. Ross and

Nisbett (1991, 193ff) use cultures to illustrate the concept of a tension system. Cultural norms, values, and ideology can provide a context of forces that affect how people construe situations and influence behavior.

As noted above, social intelligence research can expand our understanding of construal by discovering the cognitive-affective processes at work in the perception and interpretation of social situations. Germane to the understanding of social intelligence is the study of how interpersonal dynamics, cultural norms, and other factors at work in tension systems shape and influence construal processes. Social knowledge, including the knowledge of cultural norms and how to apply them in different situations, is part of the fund of knowledge that social intelligence research studies. As I will explain in section 3, social knowledge is both propositional and procedural, that is, it includes both knowledge of social norms and "how to" knowledge of how to behave in various social situations. Such social knowledge affects how people act in social situations and is one of the factors involved in tension systems. Consequently, since social intelligence research investigates construal as well as features of tension systems, it fits well with two of the three legs of Ross and Nisbett's social psychology tripod.

Finally, social intelligence research also reveals similarities between social intelligence and goal-dependent automaticity. As will be seen from the discussion of Cantor and Kihlstrom (1987) in section 3, social intelligence is goal-directed. It enables us to function well in our pursuit of goals related to life tasks. Thus, the goal-orientedness of social intelligence meshes well with goal-dependent automaticity. Moreover, it is likely that the cognitive-affective factors that constitute social intelligence become automatic or routinized in response to repeated social cues, and that some social intelligence skills, such as interpretative ability, operate below the level of conscious awareness. Here, too, there is nice fit between social intelligence as a component of personality and the cognitive-affective, goal-oriented conception of personality presupposed by automaticity researchers.

My aim in this section has been to make a case for the empirical adequacy of social intelligence research. This case has relied on two separate strands of discussion. The first strand focuses on the two main traditions in social intelligence research—idiographic and psychometric. Experiments in these traditions have confirmed and replicated results concerning the processes that constitute social intelligence. This research is empirically adequate in its own right. The second strand of my argument is that social intelligence research coheres well with other research on personality that is of interest to virtue theorists. Both strands of the argument show that social intelligence research is sufficiently robust and informative to warrant philosophical attention. In the next section, I draw on Cantor and Kihlstrom's (1987) idiographic approach, as well as results of the psychometric studies mentioned earlier, to sketch a theory of social intelligence.

3. A THEORY OF SOCIAL INTELLIGENCE

As mentioned in the introduction to this chapter, a theory of social intelligence should do two things. First, it should explain the cognitive and affective processes that constitute social intelligence. Second, it should explain how social intelligence functions in our lives.

Let us turn first to the cognitive and affective processes that comprise social intelligence. Here is an initial definition, encompassing key components of social intelligence, based on the definitions and research reviewed earlier:

> Social intelligence is a complex, multidimensional set of knowledge, skills, and abilities, comprised of perception or insight, knowledge, and behavioral ability, that, other things being equal, enables us to perform well or be successful in social or interpersonal affairs.[5]

An explanation of the elements of the definition is in order. Social perception or insight is the ability to accurately interpret verbal and nonverbal social behaviors in the context in which they occur. Perception or insight is not purely cognitive, but, as Goleman (2006, 84) suggests, likely incorporates empathetic abilities, that is, abilities to pick up on the affect or emotion that others experience. Social knowledge includes conceptual or propositional knowledge of social concepts, awareness of social norms and conventions, and procedural knowledge of how to act in various social situations. Perception or insight and knowledge are interrelated, yet conceptually distinct. Consider, for example, a picture of a young man presenting a young woman with a diamond ring. Social perception would enable an observer to decode this nonverbal social behavior, that is, to understand its meaning, by perceiving it as the custom or convention by means of which couples in Western societies have traditionally become engaged to be married. Accurate social perception of the scenario relies on knowledge of the relevant social norms and conventions. Lacking knowledge of the relevant norms and conventions, the episode is meaningless, that is, opaque to one's efforts to decode it. Consequently, social knowledge is typically necessary for one's perceptual abilities to accurately convey the meaning of social situations.

As Goleman (2006, 84) recognizes, there are degrees of social perception or insight. An insightful observer would be able not only to decode the behavior, that is, to interpret it as meaningful in light of her knowledge of relevant social conventions, but also, upon witnessing an actual ring-presenting scenario, would be able to perceive and interpret subtle, context-specific interpersonal cues. If the woman hesitates or looks doubtful, for example, an astute observer would know that she is not sure if the engagement is right for her. Similarly, an insightful observer would be able to detect hints of nervousness on the part of the man. The point is that social insight can be a more or less penetrating or fine-grained interpretative tool. More penetrating insight seems to require a greater empathetic ability to read people, that is, to pick up and interpret the emotions and attitudes of others as revealed by facial expressions and body language. Reading facial expressions and interpreting body language enables us to form mental representations of others, including representations of their mental states. Without knowledge of how to interpret facial expressions and body language, we will be unable to as readily form accurate mental representations of people, their mental states, and social episodes.

Finally, social intelligence is practical. A crucial dimension of social intelligence is behavioral ability, understood as the ability to act successfully or perform well in social situations (see Goleman 2006, 84). Social perception and knowledge contribute to this ability, which will be discussed in more detail in what follows.

Cantor and Kihlstrom's (1987) account adds to our initial understanding of social intelligence in several respects. First, they articulate in more detail the kinds of social knowledge of which social intelligence is comprised. Second, they argue that social intelligence is a form of expertise. That is, the socially intelligent person not only has and uses social knowledge effectively, she also uses the metacognitive skills of self-monitoring, planning, and evaluation to shape her social knowledge and maximize the efficacy of her actions. Related to this point is a third that addresses the second desideratum of a theory of social intelligence, namely that such a theory should explain how social intelligence works in our lives—social intelligence functions strategically to enable people to achieve goals associated with life tasks such as parenting, family life, social and civic involvement, and career pursuit. Let us examine each of these points in more detail.

Cantor and Kihlstrom's (1987) first contribution is a discussion of social knowledge. Social knowledge, as noted earlier, can be both conceptual or propositional, what they call "declarative" knowledge, and procedural, or "how to" knowledge. Though Cantor and Kihlstrom (1987) say much about the structure and organization of conceptual social knowledge that is not relevant here, one feature of this type of social knowledge bears noting: it is often "hot," or affectively laden. Concepts such as rapist and saint, for example, are valenced negatively and positively, respectively, and are often emotionally charged. Consider, too, the phrases winning the lottery, getting a parking ticket, or getting married. Our representations of these concepts elicit affect. That they do, as well as the types of affect evoked, depends on how culture or society construes these concepts, as well as on the particular social learning history of the individual, that is, on how he has come to understand these concepts through experience, upbringing, and education.

By "procedural social knowledge," Cantor and Kihlstrom (1987) do not mean the "how to" knowledge of behavioral protocols that we gain by acquaintance with social forms and conventions, for example, knowledge of how to order in a restaurant, how to act while on a date, or how to make new friends while at a party. Such procedural knowledge is clearly a part of the social knowledge repertoire, and seems necessary for socially intelligent behavior. Cantor and Kihlstrom (1987, 107), however, use "procedural social knowledge" in a different sense: to refer to the interpretative rules that people use to make sense of social experience. Unlike conceptual or declarative knowledge, which is explicitly known, we use these rules implicitly in coordination with declarative knowledge in "… perception, categorization, memory, causal attribution, judgment, and inference in both the social and the nonsocial realms" (Cantor and Kihlstrom 1987, 107–108). For example, we use a variety of "reconciliation" procedures for making sense of incongruent information about people, for instance, by inferring a cause-effect relation between incompatible attributes, as when we say that someone is hostile because he is dependent (Cantor and Kihlstrom 1987, 109).

Psychologists have discovered that people often take procedural shortcuts around the interpretative rules, even when doing so flies in the face of empirical evidence (Cantor and Kihlstrom 1987, 109). One such shortcut is the fundamental attribution error—the tendency to overattribute behavior to traits and underattribute it to situational influences. Another shortcut is the tendency to preserve personality impressions by ignoring incongruent information. Such shortcuts compromise the accuracy of our knowledge. Yet Cantor and Kihlstrom (1987, 109) are sanguine about the loss of accuracy caused by our use of procedural shortcuts, maintaining that it hardly affects the efficiency and utility of social construals. They hypothesize that shortcut rules fit well with the fuzziness of social concepts and their organization (Cantor and Kihlstrom 1987, 110).

Cantor and Kihlstrom (1987)implicitly recognize that some forms of social cognition should not be considered forms of social intelligence. They implicitly acknowledge this fact by arguing that social intelligence is a form of expertise. Expertise or proficiency in a domain is obtained through practice and the metacognitive skills of self-monitoring, planning, and evaluation. How does expertise affect knowledge? Cantor and Kihlstrom (1987, 115) point out that experts in a domain have more factual knowledge than novices and are likely to organize that knowledge in more complex and efficient ways, that is, to have interconceptual associations that allow for easy retrieval of relevant concepts as new information is acquired and interpreted. Experts process familiar information faster and with less effort than novices. Their familiarity with a domain allows them to devote greater cognitive resources to assimilating new information. However, expertise has drawbacks. Experts can become used to construing information in customary ways, and can overlook or ignore novelty, or too readily assimilate incongruent information. Though experts have their favorite ways of seeing things, they may have trouble articulating their frames of vision (Cantor and Kihlstrom 1987, 116). This feature of expertise suggests that automatic forms of cognitive processing, which occur when concepts are activated without our awareness, could occur spontaneously for experts.

The motivational involvement of experts with a domain explains their likely use of metacognitive skills. The expert may be motivated to intervene to check automatic interpretations operating outside of conscious awareness, including the use of error-prone procedural shortcuts. That is, the expert can monitor her own thinking and guide and correct potentially erroneous cognitive processing. Studies have shown that experts—those who are highly motivated and have more knowledge—are more careful and vigilant in using procedural shortcuts than non-experts, who are less personally involved or lack knowledge (Cantor and Kihlstrom 1987, 117). Moreover, studies indicate that highly motivated people generally encode information relevant to a topic more systematically, elaborately, and deeply, taking greater note of inconsistencies (Cantor and Kihlstrom 1987, 117). When motivated to do so, experts can recognize and generate alternative interpretations of situations.

The foregoing remarks on social intelligence as a form of expertise suggest an expansion of our previous definition:

> Social intelligence is a complex, multidimensional set of knowledge, skills, and abilities, comprised of perception or insight, knowledge, judgment, and behavioral ability, that are shaped and cultivated by the self-reflective activities of the agent, such as self-monitoring, planning, and evaluation. Other things being equal, social intelligence is a form of expertise that enables the agent to perform well or be successful in social or interpersonal interactions. Interest in these interactions supplies the motivation needed for the development of social intelligence.

The final piece in our emerging picture of social intelligence is furnished by Cantor and Kihlstrom's notion that social intelligence is used strategically in the pursuit of goals associated with valued life tasks. They define an individual's current life tasks as "… the set of tasks which the person sees himself or herself as working on and devoting energy to solving during a specified period in life" (Cantor and Kihlstrom 1987, 168; see also Cantor and Harlow 1994). Life tasks are the incentives for which an individual sees herself as striving—engaging, but often ill-defined, involving numerous projects and activities that change in content over the lifespan (Cantor and Kihlstrom 1987, 169–171). Life tasks are generally regarded as goods in their own right or as means by which goods can be attained. They give people's lives meaning and direction. For example, dating is a common life task at the adolescent stage of development. Achieving social and academic goals are life tasks that occupy college students. Finding marriage partners is a life task for young adults in their twenties. Parenting is a life task as families develop. Caring for elderly parents becomes a life task as adults mature and their parents age. Each of these life tasks typically occurs during a different stage of the lifespan and is influenced by cultural norms and expectations, yet is shaped by personal histories and contexts. General involvement in social life occurs almost from the cradle to the grave, from the time that children are old enough for day care to the time seniors end their days. Civic involvement spans young adulthood through senescence.

Cantor and Kihlstrom (1987, 170) do not claim, of course, that there is a fixed order in the occurrence of life tasks during the lifespan. For example, many older adults re-experience dating rituals following divorce, or set new academic and personal goals for themselves by returning to school or going to school for the first time later in life. And it is entirely possible that children, teenagers, and young adults are called upon to care for aging or ill parents. Whether life tasks occur during the life stage as generally expected in a culture or, as cultural norms are relaxed or needs arise, at different points in the lifespan, the life task frames an individual's personal goals and strategies for achieving them, and is itself framed by cultural norms and expectations.

What does it mean to say that social intelligence functions strategically in the pursuit of life tasks? Cantor and Kihlstrom (1987, 175) define a strategy as "… the set of cognitive processes that link a person's goals to his or her subsequent behavior in a life-task situation. That is, the strategy involves the ways in which the person interprets the 'problem' and plans a 'solution' so as to be consistent with his or her prevalent goals in that 'task.'" In other words, I think strategically when I think about how to act in a certain situation to achieve my intended goals, or when I frame or interpret a problem in a certain way. Strategic thinking and behavior, for Cantor and Kihlstrom, is simply goal-directed, and not necessarily manipulative or conniving (Cantor and Kihlstrom 1987, 175). The central notion in a cognitive strategy is executive control: the person has taken control of interpretations, plans, and actions with the aim of attaining a goal (Cantor and Kihlstrom 1987, 176).

Frequently used strategies often become second nature or automatic through practice. Through time and use, people can become unaware of the strategies they routinely use in interactions (Cantor and Kihlstrom 1987, 175). For example, I might discover in interactions with my spouse that potentially tense situations become defused if I adopt a calm and soothing tone of voice. This information about my spouse's reactions can function strategically in our interactions if I use it to attain my goal of keeping our interactions friendly. If repeatedly adopting a calm tone successfully maintains friendly interactions on a number of occasions, eventually, my behavior becomes routinized. I become unaware that I am using a strategy, and might even become unaware of my subtle shifts in voice tone. These shifts eventually become triggered outside of my conscious awareness by cues that communicate my spouse's tension. Thus, modulations in my voice tone can become automatic reactions to cues from my spouse that signal his or her emotional state. This is how my strategy for keeping the peace can become automatized and eventually operate below the level of conscious awareness.

The previous observations about the strategic uses of social intelligence in the pursuit of goals associated with life tasks suggests yet another amendment of the account of social intelligence:

> Social intelligence is a complex, multidimensional set of knowledge, skills, and abilities, comprised of perception or insight, knowledge, judgment, and behavioral ability, used strategically by the agent in the generally successful pursuit of goals associated with life tasks, such as family life, career pursuit, and social and civic involvement. Social intelligence is shaped and cultivated by the self-reflective activities of the agent, such as self-monitoring, planning, and evaluation and can be considered a form of expertise. Engagement with life tasks supplies the motivation needed for the development of social intelligence.

At this point, I've offered a theory of social intelligence, drawing largely on the work of Cantor and Kihlstrom (1987). The theory not only explains the cognitive-affective processes that constitute social intelligence, it also elucidates the role of social intelligence in our lives. Social intelligence makes our lives go better because it enables us to succeed in our pursuit of goals associated with life tasks. These life tasks are essential components of daily living, and are the kinds of goals that traditional eudaimonism views as indispensable for human flourishing.

Yet important questions remain unaddressed. What is the relation between social intelligence and social competence? Greenspan and Love (1997, 311) regard social intelligence as the cognitive underpinning of social competence. Other theorists, for example, Jones and Day (1997), seem to equate the two. Moreover, is social intelligence the ability to act wisely in human affairs, as Thorndike (1920) suggests?

4. SOCIAL INTELLIGENCE, SOCIAL COMPETENCE, AND SOCIAL INCOMPETENCE

What is the relation of social intelligence and social competence? It seems mistaken to think, following Greenspan and Love (1997), that social intelligence is the cognitive underpinning of social competence. It also seems wrong to simply equate the two, as do Jones and Day (1997). These views seem mistaken because they apparently jar with the commonsense meanings that attach to the terms "competence" and "intelligence." In common parlance, these are success terms, indicating that a certain standard of achievement has been met or exceeded by a particular performance. Intuitively, a performance that reflects intelligence is at a higher level of achievement than one that reflects mere competence. An intelligent performance on an exam, for example, is better than a competent performance. An intelligent, that is, deep and insightful, interpretation of Shostakovich's Fifth Symphony is better than a competent performance—one that simply gets the notes, pauses, and tempo right. Given our commonsense usage of the terms "competence" and "intelligence," it seems intuitively more plausible that social cognition is the cognitive underpinning of both social competence and social intelligence. That is, social intelligence requires roughly the same kinds of knowledge, skills, and abilities as social competence. However, in the socially intelligent person, the knowledge is deeper, more extensive, better integrated, and more readily accessible, and the skills and abilities, developed to a higher degree and used more effectively in social interaction. Following this line of thought, it makes sense to claim that having social intelligence is a greater achievement than having social competence, and one that requires some effort. This is consistent with viewing social intelligence as a form of expertise. I will sketch this view of social intelligence and social competence in this section.

Let us begin with some observations about a type of intelligence that is, perhaps, more familiar to philosophers and other academics—academic intelligence, and then extend them to the case of social intelligence. If we say that someone is academically intelligent, we are ascribing to that person knowledge as well as skill or facility in using that knowledge. Suppose we say that a student is academically intelligent in mathematics. By this we mean that she possesses content knowledge of mathematics, that is, knowledge of the axioms of geometry, for example, or of the principles of calculus, as well as procedural or "how to" knowledge specific to the discipline. If someone is academically intelligent in geometry, she not only has content knowledge of the axioms of geometry, but can process that knowledge in ways that enable her to use the axioms to solve geometrical problems, construct proofs, and derive further axioms. Moreover, the kind of processing ability she has allows her to deepen and expand her content knowledge and to apply her mathematical knowledge to other areas. In other words, when we say that someone is academically intelligent, we suggest that she has not only what researchers call "crystallized intelligence," which is a fund of acquired knowledge, but also "fluid intelligence," or the ability to think creatively and flexibly about new situations that arise in the problem domain (see Jones and Day 1996, 270–274; Lee, Wong, Day, Maxwell, and Thorpe 2000).

Academic intelligence should be distinguished from academic competence. One might think of the differences between academic intelligence and academic competence in terms of the differences between a strong "A" student and a solid "C" student. Academic competence suggests limitations in the student's potential for acquisition of knowledge and skills, as well as in her fluid intelligence, or processing abilities. An academically competent person, we think, has enough content knowledge and skill in using it to be able to get by. Her academic performance is adequate, but no more. By contrast, to say that someone is academically intelligent suggests not only a higher degree of mastery of acquired content and processing skills, but also greater potential. As noted earlier, both competence and intelligence are success terms. One cannot be said to be competent—to have earned even a grade of "C"—without having some accomplishments to one's credit. But intelligence suggests a greater measure of successful achievement, greater ability, and untapped potential.

One more term should be added to this scheme, and that is academic incompetence. To say that someone is academically incompetent in a discipline is to say that her performance falls below some minimum set of standards. She simply does not grasp the content of the discipline, nor can she use what knowledge she might have to effectively solve problems, answer questions, work out puzzles, and so on. As with academic competence, explanations of academic incompetence can vary. Perhaps the academically incompetent person lacks the natural ability to learn. Alternatively, she might have ability but lack motivation.

It should be evident that intelligent, competent, and incompetent are terms of both attribution and classification. When I say that Lauren is academically intelligent, I am attributing, on the basis of her academic performance, a certain level or degree of possession of knowledge, skills, abilities, and potential for development to her. I am also classifying her performance relative to standards of achievement.

A similar scheme of attribution and classification can be applied to the sphere of social interaction. Let us start with the notion of social incompetence. Here we can distinguish two kinds of cases. The first is illustrated by the narrator of Mark Haddon's novel, *The Curious Incident of the Dog in the Night-Time*. Early in the novel, the narrator, a fifteen-year-old autistic boy named Christopher Boone, reveals his limitations in interpreting facial expressions (Haddon 2003, 2–3). Christopher's teacher, Siobhan, presents him with a series of simple line drawings depicting faces. He can recognize and interpret only happy and sad faces, that is, line drawings with the mouth line curved either upward or downward. He is unable to decode line drawings of faces depicting more complex emotional states, such as those communicating mischievous glee, surprise, and a mix of happiness and sadness. Christopher says: "I got Siobhan to draw lots of these faces and then write down next to them exactly what they meant. I kept the piece of paper in my pocket and took it out when I didn't understand what someone was saying. But it was very difficult to decide which of the diagrams was most like the face they were making because people's faces move very quickly" (Haddon 2003, 3). Because of his impairment, the autistic boy cannot read facial expressions, and thus, is unable to communicate effectively in social interactions. He does not know what is going on. Even when given the information needed to decode the meanings of various facial expressions, he is unable to use his artificial prop as a substitute for the ability to interpret the meanings of facial expressions in actual interpersonal exchanges. Eventually, he abandons the prop and resorts to either asking people what they mean or simply walking away (Haddon 2003, 3).

Haddon's story illustrates a number of interesting points. First, because the autistic boy's inability to read faces seriously impairs his capacities to function in social situations, Christopher is rendered either socially incompetent or very near it. In a telling passage, Haddon has Christopher say: "Usually people look at you when they're talking to you. I know that they're working out what I'm thinking, but I can't tell what they're thinking" (Haddon 2003, 22). Christopher cannot pick up on and interpret social cues. Facility with reading such cues enables the rest of us to be mind-readers, that is, to have an idea of what others are thinking. Because Christopher cannot infer what others are thinking, central aspects of social life are opaque to him. Because of this opacity, he is unable to function well, and sometimes cannot function at all, in social interactions. Second, because of his autism, he will probably never possess face-reading ability to the same degree as non-autistic individuals, no matter how hard he tries to learn how to read faces or work out the meanings of other, similar social cues, such as body language. His social impairments are permanent. Finally, the story shows that the ability to interpret facial expressions is an essential and basic component of both social competence and social intelligence. What is it about reading facial expressions that is so important? As noted earlier in our discussion of social perception or insight and as suggested by the quote from Haddon's novel, interpreting facial expressions is an important ability needed to form accurate mental representations of other people and of social episodes. Our mental representations of others include conjectures about their thoughts, feelings, and motivations. This information is needed to make sense of social life. Lacking such mental representations, a person will not know what is going on and consequently, will be adrift in social interactions.

Haddon's protagonist illustrates a case in which social incompetence is due to a cognitive-affective impairment.[6] Another example will show how the failure to fully internalize social norms causes a less permanent form of social incompetence. In the film *My Fair Lady*, Eliza Doolittle is primed and prepped for a day at the races among the English upper class by Professor Henry Higgins. That is, after intense preparation, Higgins decides that Eliza is ready to make her maiden voyage among the English aristocracy. Eliza, however, is far from fully prepared, for she has not really internalized the norms regulating social interactions for that group. Her knowledge of social interactions among the English upper class is rigidly formulaic. Any departures from the code of conduct she has memorized throw her off kilter; she does not know how to handle them. She is a poor actress on stage, simulating and mimicking social forms, gestures, and mannerisms that are not natural for her. The charade ends with her outburst at the results of the race, sending a fellow spectator into a swoon.

Should Eliza care to continue her entry into the English upper crust, her plight is less serious than that of Haddon's autistic boy. Eliza can, in principle, learn the social conventions and customs of the aristocracy. She can retrain her mannerisms and learn to subdue her impulses to accord with social expectations and norms. In other words, her social incompetence is remedial, for it is in principle possible for her to develop a second nature in line with the social dictates of the English upper class. Key to the development of this second nature is the ability to form accurate mental representations of members of the aristocracy and their ways. In addition, she cannot simply view the aristocracy from an outsider's perspective, but needs to be able to understand what is going on from an insider's point of view. That is, she needs to enter the social milieu of the English upper class as a participant, and not as a spectator.

These remarks can aid us in understanding the meaning of social competence, which, as I see it, lies between social incompetence and social intelligence. The socially competent individual is part participant, and part spectator. He is engaged in social life and functions in social interactions, though not as fully or as well as he might. The socially competent individual is partially disengaged from social life or central aspects of it. His disengagement need not result from a lack of motivation. The socially competent person could want to participate in social life, yet be prevented from full or fully meaningful participation because of various deficiencies in social cognition or processing. He could be partially disengaged because he misses important aspects of the social scene—either he does not pick up on social cues at all, or he notices but misinterprets them, or, perhaps notices and interprets correctly, but does not know how to respond appropriately. Furthermore, the socially competent individual could possess a fund of social knowledge, yet lack the ability to apply this knowledge flexibly to new social situations. His disengagement might, but might not be, remediable. Perhaps, like Eliza, he lacks internalized knowledge of social norms and conventions, but could acquire this knowledge with effort. Alternatively, like Haddon's autistic child, he could be inept at picking up and interpreting socially relevant cues, and limited in his natural ability to make good the deficit. Like the academically competent "C" student, he gets by in terms of social performance, but there is much of social life that he just doesn't get. In other words, he either does not form mental representations of central aspects of social life, or forms them inaccurately, or cannot fluidly apply to new situations the representations he is able to form.

By contrast, the socially intelligent person is engaged with social life as a full participant. Her level of engagement is made possible by the fact that she is able to form accurate mental representations of social life on the basis of which she makes judgments and acts. By and large, she is able to read people accurately, and has the knowledge of norms and conventions needed to make sense of social interactions and episodes. She is able to use her skills to advance goals, and can apply her fund of social knowledge across various social domains, flexibly extrapolating to new situations she encounters. Viewing social intelligence as a form of expertise helps us to understand how the socially intelligent person has come by her abilities: she has taken the time and made the effort to monitor her interactions, evaluate her social performances, and plan her actions. Natural ability plays a part in her expertise, but, like the academically intelligent student, she works to develop and maintain her social intelligence. This willingness to work at being socially intelligent requires a fairly high level of motivation.

What practical steps might someone take to cultivate social intelligence? Here are some examples. Developing attentiveness to others is a very basic step. If a person is self-absorbed and oblivious to those around her, she can hardly pick up on social cues and participate fully in social life. Another basic step is learning how to correctly interpret the cues she receives from others. Learning how to interpret social stimuli can involve a certain degree of acuity, but is important because correct interpretation allows us to be in sync with others—to follow the flow of interpersonal dynamics. Learning how to interpret social stimuli correctly involves getting to know other people, including the cultural backgrounds that shape their perceptions and behavior. For example, if I wish to get along well with my new Muslim neighbors who have just immigrated from Pakistan, I should find out about their culture so that I can understand how to best interact with them, or, at least, how to avoid inadvertently causing offense. Finally, monitoring one's own reactions, at least in certain situations, is an important part of developing social intelligence. One who simply blurts out whatever comes to mind during a sensitive conversation, for example, does not display social intelligence. Of course, we all sometimes blurt things out or react spontaneously to social stimuli, and spontaneous reactions are not always bad. A socially intelligent response, however, is more measured, and is calibrated to achieve one's goals in the situation at hand. Interpersonal interactions typically go more smoothly with than without social intelligence.

Could the socially intelligent person be disengaged from social life because he is unmotivated to participate? We can easily imagine a person who has all of the cognitive-affective prerequisites for socially intelligent behavior but chooses not to engage in it. He is the opposite of the socially competent individual who wants to participate fully in social life, but lacks the necessary cognitive-affective prerequisites. Would we call the equipped but unmotivated person socially intelligent? I would say "yes," provided that the individual in question could immediately produce socially intelligent behavior if he wanted to. That is, his social intelligence is fully developed but unused. Because he could immediately produce socially intelligent behavior if he wanted to, I am inclined to say that he is, indeed, socially intelligent.

In real life, the lines between social intelligence, competence, and incompetence are not hard and fast. A person can be competent on some occasions or in some domains of social life, such as work-related matters, while being incompetent in others, such as romantic relationships or friendships. Competence and incompetence are often matters of degrees of ability to function in various types of social situations. Similarly, a person could be socially intelligent in some domains, but only socially competent in others. Consider a mother who, after many years of child-rearing and working in the home, re-enters the workforce. At first, at least, she is likely to be only socially competent in the workplace in the sense that she will not be able to function socially as well at work as at home. However, we might think that her initial social deficits in the workplace are due only to a lack of knowledge of workplace norms, and that the cognitive skills and abilities that enable her to function well in family life can be adapted to the domain of career pursuits. In other words, the socially intelligent person's cognitive-affective processes, such as perception or insight and judgment, should be sufficiently well developed and flexible so that, with attention and practice, they can be adapted for use across different social domains, just as the analytical reasoning skills suited to one domain, such as mathematical problem-solving, can be adapted for use in a different domain, such as chess-playing. In addition, the metacognitive skills of the socially intelligent person—for example, her ability to step back and critically analyze social situations, to learn lessons from her experiences, and to use that feedback in other social encounters—should help her to adjust her skills to domain differences. If so, shortcomings in socially intelligent behavior that occur in a new domain should be, for the socially intelligent person, correctible.

An interesting question is how traits such as introversion and extraversion affect the cognitions and motivations needed for social intelligence. Extraverted people are naturally outgoing and interested in social affairs, whereas introverts tend to be shier and more inwardly focused. Does it follow that extraverts are more likely to be socially intelligent than introverts? I think not. Introverts can certainly be observant of social affairs, conversant with social norms and conventions, and insightful in reading people and picking up on social cues. Introverts can also care deeply about social life. For example, introverted parents do not love their children any less than extraverted parents simply because they are introverted, and can take just as much of an interest in their children's lives and social affairs as extraverted parents do. Introverts can be as fully engaged, both cognitively and motivationally, with social life as extraverts. The main difference between the socially intelligent behavior of introverts and extraverts, I think, is style. One can be quietly socially intelligent, deeply invested in social affairs, and fully engaged.

At this point, we should have an idea of why social intelligence matters. Social intelligence matters because it enables us to perform well in social life—to interact with others as knowledgeable and engaged social participants, and to advance and achieve valued goals associated with life tasks. Social intelligence, it seems, is necessary for living well. Without it, we lead diminished social lives.

5. SOCIAL INTELLIGENCE AND WISDOM

Following Thorndike (1920), is it correct to think that social intelligence is the ability to act wisely in human affairs? To address this question, we need to ask what is meant by wisdom and acting wisely. Three different interpretations of the meanings of these terms spring to mind. First, we can think of a pre-theoretical, colloquial sense of wisdom and of acting wisely for which wisdom and wise action are correlated with goodness. To act wisely in human affairs is to act with goodness. Second, we might interpret wisdom to mean practical wisdom in Aristotle's sense: roughly, the ability to discern situations that call for virtuous response, know the actions that are appropriate in those situations, and know how to act accordingly. In general, practical wisdom is the ability to reason well about practical matters. Finally, wisdom could be interpreted to mean a higher level of knowledge about what is really important in life or deeper insight into the human heart, as is said to be possessed by sages and other enlightened persons in some Asian philosophical traditions, such as Buddhism (see Kupperman 2005, 255–258).

Is social intelligence simply equivalent to acting wisely in human affairs, where this connotes acting with goodness? Sternberg (1998, 359) neatly distinguishes social intelligence from wisdom: "Social intelligence can be applied to understanding and getting along with others, to any ends, for any purposes. Wisdom seeks out a good through a balancing of interests." Sternberg is certainly correct about social intelligence. Except for Goleman (2006, 11–12, 84), social intelligence theorists generally do not suggest that social intelligence must entail a concern for others' interests, or cannot involve the manipulation of others for personal gain or evil ends. Wisdom, by contrast, seems to be widely recognized as in some sense correlated with or connected with goodness. Consequently, social intelligence is not equivalent to wisdom in the pre-theoretical or colloquial sense in which wisdom is associated with goodness.

Is social intelligence equivalent to practical wisdom in Aristotle's sense? I think that social intelligence is not equivalent to practical wisdom, though it is similar to it in some respects. Very roughly, we can say that practical wisdom includes skills of discernment—the abilities to discern the morally salient features of situations, as well as appropriately virtuous responses—and, in general, the wherewithal to deliberate well about practical matters. Certainly Aristotle includes as part of being virtuous having appropriate feelings or emotions; consequently, I would say that emotional sensitivity is included in Aristotle's conception of practical wisdom. Social intelligence also includes these elements—perceptual abilities, cognitive processing, the general ability to reason and judge well in social matters, and emotional and empathic sensitivity to others.[7]

Despite these similarities, social intelligence and practical wisdom are not equivalent. For one thing, I see social intelligence as going beyond practical wisdom in its emphasis on empathic sensitivity to others. More importantly, however, social intelligence need not be associated with virtue, but can be used for morally neutral or bad ends. In many situations, social intelligence could amount to what Aristotle calls cleverness – the ability to reason well, though not virtuously. Consequently, social intelligence and practical wisdom are not equivalent.

Is social intelligence equivalent to sage-like wisdom, such as that advocated as an ideal by some Asian traditions, such as Buddhism? Wisdom in the senses extolled in these traditions seems to be a higher form of knowledge into what is meaningful or valuable in human life that allows us insight into the human heart. It is acquired through meditation that focuses inward and seeks to empty the mind of thoughts and sensations, thereby simply letting ourselves "be." Wisdom gives rise to certain personal qualities, such as poise, equanimity, patience, self-control, and the absence of cravings and strong, afflictive emotions (Kupperman 2006, 56–57; His Holiness the Dalai Lama 1999, 81–131). Wisdom leads not only to goodness, but to calm and inner peace (Kupperman 2001, 22–39). Social intelligence is clearly not equivalent to wisdom in this sense, though I believe it has interesting affinities with aspects of this kind of wisdom.

Here is how. Sometimes, the search for a measure of sage-like wisdom, as well as the search for social intelligence, occurs during or after a period of breakdown or crisis. An important relationship, perhaps a friendship or a marriage, has gone bad. We are bereft and adrift, feeling that we have bungled our chances for happiness, and that we are bad or unworthy people who will continue making the same kinds of mistakes unless we undertake some serious soul-searching and reshaping of self. From a social intelligence perspective, we need to examine and evaluate our relationships, asking ourselves where we missed important signals from the other, how we might improve our sensitivities, how we might be aware of our weaknesses, and how we might manage our relationships more effectively in the future. As I understand them, the kinds of meditative or contemplative practices prescribed by Buddhism, for example, advocate a reflective yet nonevaluative "being with" ourselves and an openness to experiencing our emotions and relationships as they are, warts, pain, and all (Chodron 2005). This "being with" ourselves, our emotions, and our relationships, allows us a way of seeing ourselves and our social world that is not entirely dissimilar from the more overtly analytic outlook afforded by taking a social intelligence approach.[8] Each perspective allows us a different way of examining and of understanding ourselves and our relationships. If successful, the result of each type of processing of information about self and relationships is a kind of personal growth and healthier way of being and functioning.

6. CONCLUSION

This chapter has been devoted to exploring social intelligence. I've explained what social intelligence is, and have argued that social intelligence research is important and of interest to virtue theorists. I've also advanced a theory of social intelligence that identifies the cognitive-affective processes that constitute it and how social intelligence functions in our lives. Social intelligence, as sketched in this chapter, is a complex constellation of conceptual and procedural knowledge and cognitive-affective abilities that enable us to be full and effective participants in social life. Social intelligence, in short, enables us to live well—to be fully engaged with the social worlds we inhabit. Since virtue also enables us to live well, it is worth asking whether and how social intelligence is related to virtue. In the next chapter, I argue that virtue is a form of social intelligence. To show that virtue is a form of social intelligence situates virtue squarely within yet another empirical research tradition in psychology, and is the final plank in the overall project of articulating an empirically grounded theory of virtue.

4

VIRTUE AS SOCIAL INTELLIGENCE

1. INTRODUCTION

In the last chapter, I explained the notion of social intelligence—it is constituted by a complex panoply of cognitive-affective processes, and it helps people in social living. Virtues, as traditionally conceived, are also constituted by the same kinds of cognitive-affective elements and processes that constitute social intelligence, and like social intelligence, enable us to pursue goals associated with valued life tasks. What is the relation of virtue and social intelligence? Having social intelligence can help us to achieve any goals of social living—good, bad, or neutral (see Sternberg 1998, 359). Virtues, however, will not help us to advance any social goals, but only a subset of these. In this chapter, I claim that virtues are forms of social intelligence, and argue that the motivations characteristic of virtues distinguish them from other forms of social intelligence.

To make good the claim that the motivations characteristic of virtues distinguish them from other forms of social intelligence, a structural claim about virtue must be defended. The claim is this: virtues, modeled on CAPS (cognitive-affective processing system) traits, are tightly integrated bundles of distinctive motivations, cognitions, and affective elements, in which the cognitive and affective components are shaped and directed by the motivations characteristic of virtue. The structural claim about virtue is introduced in section 2, and elaborated and defended in section 3. In section 4, I use an extended example to illustrate how social intelligence theory explains virtuous and vicious behavior. In section 5,

I address additional questions about the use of social intelligence theory in explaining virtue.

2. WHAT DOES IT MEAN TO SAY THAT VIRTUE IS A FORM OF SOCIAL INTELLIGENCE?

Sternberg (1998, 359) contends that social intelligence can be used for any ends—morally good, bad, or neutral. Among the ends for which social intelligence can be used are those of virtue. Put another way, we can say that social intelligence can be driven by many kinds of motivations, among which are the motivations characteristic of virtue. Virtues are distinctive as forms of social intelligence because of their distinctive motivations.

To show that virtue is a form of social intelligence, we must defend the structural claim that virtues are complex constellations of cognitive, motivational, and affective elements, in which the cognitive elements are deeply shaped and influenced by the motivational components. That is, in the psychology of the virtuous agent, the motivations intrinsic to virtue shape the perceptions, thoughts, and judgments also intrinsic to virtue such that, were the motivations to be removed from the agent's psychological economy or replaced with others, the perceptions, thoughts, and judgments would also change. These motives shape the cognitive elements intrinsic to the virtues and render them separate forms of social intelligence that differ from those types of social intelligence in which knowledge, cognitive processes, and affective sensitivities are influenced by morally neutral, self-interested, or malicious motives. In other words, the virtuous person's motivations—her desire to be virtuous or to advance a virtue-relevant goal—shape her perceptions of situations and, more generally, how she sees people and the world. Influenced by her virtuous motivations, the virtuous person's perceptions, cognitions, and affective sensitivities function together to enable the agent to act virtuously in the pursuit of goals associated with life tasks. Were the virtuous person's motivations to be removed or replaced, her perceptions, cognitions, and affective sensitivities would also change. Thus, the virtues are distinctive kinds of social intelligence that are distinguished from other types through the power of virtuous motivation to shape and direct other constituent elements of the virtues. The structural claim is a conceptual assertion about how the constituent elements of a virtue must fit together both if it is to be a virtue in the traditional Aristotelian sense and if it is to be a form of social intelligence.

My stress on the motivations of the virtuous person is not meant to deny the role of certain distinctive normative beliefs in constituting virtues. Virtues are distinguishable from other forms of social intelligence by reference to these distinctive normative beliefs—a virtuous person might believe that another is suffering and that she deserves help. Yet the fact that these normative beliefs play the role they do, I contend, is because they've been directed by the virtuous person's motivations. Consider someone who believes that another is suffering and needs help. In the compassionate person, this belief plays the normative role it does because of the person's compassionate motivations. It is possible for someone to have formed the belief that another is suffering and deserves help, yet be unmotivated to act on it, or be motivated to act viciously in the circumstances—to see the situation as an occasion to take advantage of the other's plight. Consequently, I stress the virtuous person's motivations because of their influence in shaping and directing other distinctive elements that constitute virtue. This all too brief explanation will be amplified in section 3.

3. THE STRUCTURAL CLAIM ELABORATED AND DEFENDED

As noted, the notion that virtues (and some vices) can be types of social intelligence rests on a structural claim about virtue: that the virtues are well-integrated bundles or configurations of motivations, cognitions, and affective sensitivities in which the motivations characteristic of specific virtues shape and influence the other elements. Why think that this claim is true?

To motivate the structural claim, we need briefly to revisit a debate about the kinds of psychological states that can produce action, including virtuous action. McDowell (1979) believes the virtuous person sees the world a certain way. He explains the virtuous person's perspective by invoking a conception of virtues as forms of knowledge—sensitivities that enable virtuous agents to respond to the requirements of situations. This knowledge is complex, consisting of a conception of what virtuous life requires as well as perceptual awareness of what virtue demands in specific circumstances, but it is not motivationally inert. In other words, McDowell argues for a conception of the motivational state of the virtuous agent as unitary.[1]

The notion that virtues could be forms of knowledge that motivate is amenable to the claim that virtues are types of social intelligence. Why not use McDowell's conception to argue that virtues are forms of social intelligence? McDowell's view has been criticized. Smith (1994, 116–125), for example, maintains that action-producing psychological states are not unitary, but consist of separable belief-like states and desire-like states.

Smith makes a Humean claim: it is always possible, Smith (1994, 119) thinks, for "... agents who are in some particular belief-like state not to be in some particular desire-like state ..." The Humean claim is a powerful one. It always seems possible for someone to believe that a particular action is morally required but not be motivated to perform it. This could be true of a virtuous agent under some circumstances. A virtuous agent could, for example, suffer from depression or some other condition that saps motivation while leaving cognition intact (Smith 1994, 120). According to the Humean picture, then, motivation does not depend on beliefs alone, but requires an agent's having desires as well as beliefs. If we are drawn to the Humean view of motivation and we believe that virtues are intrinsically motivating, we must abandon the notion that virtues are solely forms of knowledge. The psychological state of the virtuous agent must be analyzed at least in terms of belief-like states and desire-like states, and perhaps in terms of other variables.

Handling the Humean view presents the defender of virtue as social intelligence with two problems. The first is that of describing the structure of virtue in a way that affords insight into action-producing psychological states of virtuous agents. The second is that the Humean view challenges the structural claim about virtue as social intelligence. The challenge is to show how the psychological state of the virtuous agent could not be unitary, that is, could consist of different kinds of states, such as belief-like states and desire-like states, yet the structure of virtue could be sufficiently well-integrated to make it plausible to think that virtues are distinctive forms of social intelligence, separate from other forms. In other words, if the beliefs and desires constitutive of virtues are only contingently related and can always pull apart, why not think that the social intelligence components of virtues are also only contingently related to virtuous motivations—that the social intelligence and motivational elements of virtue also easily pull apart? If this is possible, it would be mistaken to think that virtues are distinctive forms of social intelligence in which the social intelligence elements are deeply shaped by the motivations distinctive of the virtues, such that, were the motivations to be removed or replaced, the social intelligence components would also be changed.

To address the first issue and get a framework for approaching the second, let us refer to the CAPS conception of traits. This conception furnishes a useful way of thinking about virtuous dispositions and enables us to explain the virtuous person's perspective. A brief review of the main features of the CAPS conception will be useful.

According to the CAPS view, traits are networks of frequently activated, mutually influencing variables. We should recall that the components of this system are social-cognitive units—variables such as beliefs, desires, feelings, expectations, values, and self-regulatory plans. The variables are activated in response to features of situations or internal stimuli such as the thoughts of the agent. Encountering someone in distress, for example, can cause me to feel sorrow for her plight, activate the belief that I should help, trigger my desire to help, and set in motion plans to offer aid. These components constitute a compassionate response to the distress of the other. The repeated activation of sets of variables over time results in relatively stable dispositions. Moreover, perceptions matter for CAPS traits. Mischel and Shoda (1995), the authors of the CAPS conception, maintain that people interpret the stimuli they respond to: an agent's subjective construals of the objective features of situations are important for understanding her behavior. My dispositions influence the categories I use to interpret situational stimuli; these interpretations then reinforce dispositions.

As an aside, we should note how social intelligence is relevant to the interpretative aspect of CAPS traits. A socially intelligent person has reflected on and developed her skills of interpretation and response, curtailing or inhibiting those she regards as negative, and cultivating those she regards as positive and useful. The socially intelligent person monitors and manages her interpretations and reactions. She is not simply at the mercy of external stimuli, but is able, to some extent, to shape her interpretations and reactions and control how things affect her. She can thereby influence her character. In other words, social intelligence facilitates the kinds of self-shaping of traits and character suggested at the end of chapter 1, where I offered an explanation from the psychology of prejudice of how negative traits might be inhibited and positive traits, cultivated. To be sure, the socially intelligent person is also able to use her interpretations and reactions to advance goals other than the cultivation of character. These socially intelligent reactions can become routinized in the manner described in chapter 2, where goal-dependent automaticity was discussed as an empirical framework for understanding habitual virtuous actions. Social intelligence enables people to shape themselves, pursue their goals, and influence their social world, both consciously and nonconsciously.

These remarks shed light on how virtue is a form of social intelligence. If someone is committed to virtue cultivation, say, to becoming a more compassionate, caring person, she will go through essentially the same kind of self-monitoring and self-management as the socially intelligent person. As she cultivates her virtue and it becomes second nature to her, her virtuous disposition will cause her to see or interpret the world in certain ways. Her disposition influences the categories she uses to process information and her responses to situations.

Let us rejoin the discussion of CAPS. The CAPS analysis of traits is useful for understanding the action-producing psychological states of virtuous agents. According to the CAPS account, the mutual interaction and reinforcement of activated variables over time creates a relatively stable psychological structure, the trait or virtue, which guides and shapes information processing and responses to situations. If the variables that constitute the trait structure are frequently activated, they become chronically accessible, that is, readily activated in response to situational features. We can then say that the agent is disposed to act in certain ways in response to certain stimuli—for example, compassionately in response to the distress of others, or courageously in response to perceived threats.

This conception of traits and virtues as relatively stable structures of linked, frequently activated variables allows us to address the Humean view's challenge to the structural claim about virtue. That is the challenge of explaining how the psychological state of the virtuous agent can be non-unitary, that is, consisting of belief-like states and desire-like states, yet the virtue itself can be sufficiently well-integrated to be a form of social intelligence.

I believe the CAPS conception allows us to see how the psychological state of the fully virtuous agent can be nonunitary, yet its elements tightly integrated in such a way that they cannot easily pull apart, as on the Humean view. The motivational variables that partially constitute the structure of virtues, I believe, exert considerable influence over the cognitive variables. In other words, the motives and desires that partially constitute virtues shape the cognitions, cognitive processes, and affective sensitivities that are also integral to virtues. We can see this by contrasting the terms in which the virtuous "see" or interpret the world with those in which the vicious "see" it.

Perceiving another in distress, the virtuous person is compassionately moved by his misfortune and desires to help. Being moved and desiring to help suggest interpretative categories that guide the virtuous person's construals of the other: as a victim of misfortune and potential recipient of assistance. By contrast, the cruel person's motivations lead her to see the distress of another in very different terms—perhaps as the occasion for malicious fun. According to this line of reasoning, the initial categories used by the compassionate and the cruel person are shaped by their virtue and vice. The compassionate person simply sees the other as a person in need of help. The cruel person need not see the other as a person in need at all. Instead, if her cruelty is deeply ingrained, she may see the other as a potential object of fun.

An alternative way of describing the compassionate and cruel person's initial perceptions of the other is that both could use the same interpretative category to shape their initial construal of the other—both could categorize the other as someone in need of help. However, even if their initial categorization of the other is the same, their further interpretations and reactions will be colored by their respective trait-based motivations: the compassionate person interprets the other in need of help as a potential recipient of aid; the cruel person construes the other as a potential object of malicious enjoyment. In other words, in the virtuous person, the initial categorization of the other as a person in need of help activates the variables that constitute her trait of compassion—sympathy for the other, the desire to help, and so on. By contrast, in the vicious person, the initial classification of the other as a person in need of help triggers the variables that form her trait of cruelty—indifference toward the other's plight and the desire to take advantage of the occasion for her own fun.

Similarly, if a person is generous, her trait of generosity shapes how she responds to the objects she classifies as her possessions—her desires to give and to share shape how she sees her possessions—as resources to be shared or used in common, and not, as the stingy person sees the objects she categorizes as her belongings, as scarce goods to be hoarded or kept from others. If a person is courageous, her self-confidence and fearlessness cause her to see events or situations she might initially classify as obstacles not as the cowardly person would see them—as threats or insurmountable impediments—but as challenges that will develop her strengths and skills.

The point is that virtues (and vices) are complex wholes consisting of interrelations of different kinds of variables. When a virtue is activated by a stimulus, say, by seeing another in need, the motivational variables that are integral components of the virtue (or vice) influence the activation of other variables, including cognitions and affective responses, thereby shaping a kind of entrainment of activated linked variables. If the motivations intrinsic to virtues were removed or replaced, the other variables activated in the entrainment would also change.

Thus, the CAPS account of trait structure and dynamics gives us insight into the psychological state of the virtuous agent. If the account is correct, the psychological state of the virtuous agent is complex. If the agent has the desires and motivations intrinsic to virtue, I've argued, these motivational elements deeply influence her beliefs and affective responses. How does this claim mesh with Smith's contention that it is always possible for "... agents who are in some particular belief-like state not to be in some particular desire-like state ..." (Smith 1994, 119)? It is true, I think, that if someone is in a particular belief-like state, for example, if she believes that another person is in need of aid, it is possible for her not to be in some particular desire-like state, such as the state of desiring to help. In an indifferent person, the belief that someone needs help need not activate any desire. The indifferent person could believe that another needs help, and also believe that this is no concern of hers. In a cruel person, the belief that someone needs help could activate the desire to have fun at the other's expense. Of course, it is also possible that there are persons in whom the belief that another needs help activates the desire to help. I agree with Smith that if someone is in a particular belief-like state, it is a contingent matter whether she is also in a particular desire-like state.

My claim is that the belief that someone is in need of help will, other things being equal, activate a particular desire-like state in a compassionate person—namely, the state of being moved to help. The activation of the desire-like state of being moved to help then triggers other belief-like states, such as the states of believing that the person who is the target of her compassion is suffering, requires particular kinds of assistance, requires it now, requires it from her, and so on. It does not make sense for her to compassionately desire to help someone unless she also believes that the other needs help.[2] The terms in which she views the other whom she believes to be in need are influenced by her compassionate desire. In other words, if a person is genuinely in a particular desire-like state, such as the state of being compassionately moved, it would be unintelligible for her not to be in a particular belief-like state regarding the need of the other for help.

To say this is compatible with admitting that someone can have a particular belief, such as the belief that another needs help, without necessarily being motivated to act on it, and that someone can be mistaken in her belief that another needs help, yet be genuinely motivated to act on it. It is also compatible with weakness of will, that is, with the person believing that the other needs help and desiring to help, yet being insufficiently motivated to act on her desire. Finally, it is compatible with a virtuous person's suffering from depression or some other condition that saps motivation but leaves cognition intact.

Two explanations of how depression can affect the virtuous person's motivation seem likely. According to the first, the depressed virtuous person would still be able to believe that another needs help, that is, her ability to categorize others as persons in need of help would remain intact despite her depression, but these beliefs would not trigger her compassionate motivations or the beliefs that are shaped by them. In this kind of case, the virtuous person's trait-based desires and the beliefs colored by them are suppressed by her depression; her compassion is not activated. Alternatively, the depressed virtuous person's cognitions remain intact; as in the preceding scenario, she believes that another needs help. Yet such beliefs have so frequently activated her compassion in the past that triggerings of her compassionate motives are now routinized. Consequently, despite her depression, her belief that another needs help automatically activates her compassionate desire to help. At this point, we have two possibilities. Either the depressed virtuous person acts or she does not. If she acts, then the force of the depression is not strong enough to overcome the strength of her automatically activated desire to help. If she does not act, it is likely that the depression overcomes the action-guiding force of her compassionate desires. In other words, her trait of compassion is activated, but is weakened by the enervating force of her depression.

To recap the story so far, according to the CAPS account, the virtuous person's perspective can be explained at the level of psychological processing in terms of the interaction of mutually influencing, linked variables that become relatively stable dispositions through repeated activation over time. In particular, the virtuous person's perspective is explained in terms of the influence that her motivations exert over her beliefs and cognitive processes. The virtuous person becomes used to seeing the world in particular ways—ways that are deeply influenced by her virtuous motivations. Were these motivations to change, that is, to be removed from the agent's psychological economy or replaced by other motivations, her trait-based interpretative categories and cognitive processes would change also. Consequently, the virtuous person's perspective is explained by a conception of virtues as well-integrated cognitive-motivational-affective wholes. These wholes are forms of social intelligence that are separate and distinguishable from other forms because of the effect that virtuous motivations have in influencing the other elements of virtue.

4. HOW VIRTUE FUNCTIONS AS SOCIAL INTELLIGENCE

We can illustrate how virtue functions as social intelligence by means of an extended example. In *On Personality*, Goldie (2004, 43–47) beautifully illustrates how virtues and vices affect agents' goals in interpersonal interactions, as well as the means taken to achieve those ends. The vignette is one in which four friends meet to celebrate another's birthday. Trisha has turned thirty, and Susan, Charles, Ian, and Lucy are having a celebratory dinner with her. The setting is a restaurant. The friends have been teasing Trisha about her age. At first, she does not mind, but as the teasing goes on, she becomes upset and is close to tears. The different reactions of each friend to Trisha's state are telling. Susan, by hypothesis, displays the virtue of kindness. In the following analysis, I contrast Susan's responses with those of the other members of the dinner party to illustrate how social intelligence theory would portray what the kind person does, as well as describe various forms of vice.

As the teasing goes on, Susan notices Trisha's plight and reacts with kindness by discreetly changing the subject. In Goldie's words, "Susan quickly becomes aware that Trisha is going to cry, and, with characteristic sensitivity, sees what ought to be done, and does it" (2004, 44). Susan's kindness is a good example of virtue as social intelligence. Her kindness is social intelligence because it guides her reactions to produce an outcome that successfully advances a virtue-relevant social goal, namely, comforting her friend. Simply changing the subject diverts everyone's attention from the irritating factor and gives Trisha the opportunity to refocus and calm down.

Furthermore, Susan's kindness is a form of social intelligence because it embodies the social know-how necessary to manage the situation in a way that produces the desired result. Susan has many options for action that might aim at achieving the goal of comforting Trisha. Goldie (2004, 44) suggests, for example, that Susan could put her arm around Trisha and apologize for the teasing. He also remarks that this would not be the right thing to do. Such an action in a public setting would no doubt upset and embarrass Trisha even more. In other words, Susan's kindness is imbued with practical wisdom, and is not simply cleverness. As Goldie (2004, 44) puts it, Susan's "... kindness, her sensitivity, and her practical wisdom (her common sense) just enable her to appreciate what should be done in this particular case." I suggest that she appreciates what needs to be done and is able to do it because her kindness is social intelligence. Susan has the perceptions, knowledge, judgment, and behavioral ability needed to act effectively in the situation, shaped and guided in the service of a social goal by the motivations characteristic of kindness. By contrast, someone who tries to comfort Trisha by putting an arm around her and apologizing would succeed neither in being kind nor in being socially intelligent. Her attempt at kindness would fall short precisely because it lacks an element common to both social intelligence, and, in the circumstances, practical wisdom—an awareness of the kinds of behavior that can effectively comfort someone in distress and of the kinds that compound embarrassment in public situations.

As a final comment on Susan, we should note that her goal of alleviating her friend's distress is dictated by her kindness. If she is a kind person, she will have a virtue-relevant goal in the situation, which influences how she perceives the situation, what she wants to do about it, and how she acts.

Charles is another participant in the scenario. Like Susan, Charles notices that Trisha is close to tears, but instead of seeing that fact as a reason to stop the teasing, he sees it as a reason to continue until she breaks down. Charles, Goldie (2004, 45) writes, "... wants to have some fun at her expense." I would say that Charles has the vice of cruelty and that this vice is a form of social intelligence in the situation. Why is Charles's cruelty a form of social intelligence? His vicious motivation influences his perceptions and goals. He correctly judges that Trisha is close to tears, but, unlike Susan, he interprets it as an opportunity to attain the malicious goal of having fun at Trisha's expense. Charles sees the situation in terms dictated by his cruelty. Charles's vice is a form of social intelligence because it enables him to correctly perceive the situation and provides him with the social know-how to manipulate it in the service of his desired end. As we will see in a moment, Charles's cruelty also results in his manipulating another friend at the table to advance his mean-spirited goal.

Both Susan and Charles see facts about their friend's emotional state as reasons for acting, though as reasons to act in very different ways. That their interpretations of facts about Trisha's state yield such different reasons for acting is due to their use of different interpretative categories. Both categorize Trisha as a friend close to tears, but each shapes this initial categorization in a different way owing to the differences in their motivations. Susan's kindness causes her to categorize Trisha as a friend-close-to-tears-in-need-of-rescue, or something of the sort. Charles's cruelty causes him to interpret Trisha as a friend-close-to-tears-and-possible-object-of-malicious-fun or something similar. As argued in section 3, the motivations characteristic of virtue and vice, respectively, dictate the interpretative categories in terms of which each person sees and understands the world. Kindness and cruelty, and by extension, virtue and vice, are forms of social intelligence because they incorporate distinctively shaped cognitions and cognitive processes. Such virtues and vices are used strategically by agents in social situations to pursue life-task related goals, such as engaging in social life and forming and maintaining friendships.

Several more comments on Goldie's example merit mention. Ian, another guest at the dinner party, continues teasing Trisha because he does not notice her emotional state. According to Goldie (2004, 46), Ian is not unpleasant like Charles, but is inconsiderate: he lacks the virtue of kindness and considerateness for others. Does Ian have a vice? Goldie (2004, 46) thinks not. He claims that Ian is not morally bad, but at a moral zero. However, I think that Ian is culpable of a vice: a morally objectionable obliviousness to others. Ian, we might say, is "thick" or obtuse.

There are two options for further analysis of Ian's state. One is that Ian has capacities for social intelligence the operation of which have been blocked or inhibited in the circumstances. Ian's capacities for empathetic engagement could be temporarily blocked, or his perceptual abilities could be narrowed in the situation at hand due to misfocused or inadequate attention on his part. Since Trisha's state is obvious to the others present, these explanations of Ian are unconvincing. Consequently, I tend to think that the other option for analyzing Ian is more promising: he simply lacks the social intelligence needed to register and interpret the obvious cues that Trisha is close to tears.

Why might he lack these social skills and abilities? One possibility among others is that he lacks them because he has not been motivated enough to acquire them. If someone is so disengaged from social life that he does not bother to develop basic social skills, this fact suggests that the individual in question might be guilty of undue self-absorption or self-centeredness. If so, Ian's inconsiderateness is a vice. Of course, this is not the only possible explanation of his lack of social intelligence. Ian could suffer from social deficits through no fault of his own, as is the case with high-functioning autistics and those suffering from Asberger syndrome. Lack of appropriate attention to others due to these causes is not really inconsiderateness, and hence, is not a vice.

Finally, let's consider Lucy, the fourth friend at the table. Lucy, as Goldie describes her, notices that Trisha is close to tears, and at first sees this as a reason to stop the teasing. However, Charles, again using cruelty as social intelligence, whispers nonsensical psychobabble to the gullible Lucy, thereby manipulating her into believing that Trisha has a deep unconscious longing to be teased and brought to tears in front of her friends. Goldie (2004, 46) writes that Lucy's gullibility is an intellectual vice—the disposition to believe what one is told on the basis of inadequate evidence. The story of how Lucy's gullibility affects her behavior toward Trisha shows, Goldie thinks, how intellectual vices harm not just their possessor, but others as well (2004, 46–47). Conversely, he claims, intellectual virtues can be useful and helpful to others (2004, 47).

I think a slightly different slant on Lucy is interesting to explore. She obviously trusts Charles inappropriately. Perhaps, then, her gullibility is due in part to inappropriate trust. If so, her gullibility is not just an intellectual vice with moral implications. It is related to a moral character flaw—the flaw of being too trusting. This vice is explicable by reference to social intelligence. People who are too trusting or too naïve lack social savvy, and thus are easy marks for the unscrupulous. In other words, the lack of adequate knowledge of whom to trust and of how to detect signs of an untrustworthy character is a lack of social intelligence. So Lucy's gullibility might not be only the intellectual vice of being insufficiently skeptical or exacting in standards of evidence. It could also be the moral vice of being too trusting, which bespeaks a lack of adequate social intelligence.

To sum up, viewing virtue and vice as forms of social intelligence furnishes us with a fresh perspective on a familiar topic. Analyzing Goldie's

(2004) example illustrates not only how virtues and vices can be forms of social intelligence, but also shows how they are used in that capacity in everyday social interactions. We can now see how some forms of behavior and the dispositions that produce them, such as obliviousness to others and inappropriate trust, can be morally vicious, and why: because their possessors lack social intelligence. The landscape of virtues and vices and their relations to social intelligence is complex. In the next section of this chapter, I'll address some remaining questions.

5. REMAINING QUESTIONS

A first question is this: aren't some virtues, such as temperance and humility, harder to explain than others on the social intelligence model? One might think this, I suppose, because these virtues are self-regarding, as contrasted with other-directed virtues, such as courage or benevolence. To be sure, temperance and humility are self-regarding in the sense that they are about the agent—about how she regulates her desires for food, drink, sex, and the like, and about her attitudes toward her strengths and achievements. Yet there are good social reasons for being both temperate and humble. In other words, being temperate and humble can help make the agent's life go better in a social sense. Consider, for example, how rude and tiresome people who are intemperate about food and drink can be at a party, or how a spouse who is intemperate about sex can ruin a marriage. Consider, too, how difficult it is to live and work with people who are arrogant and conceited, who lack proper humility. The preceding observations show, I think, that temperance and humility are easily explained by the social intelligence model. They make our lives go better by making us pleasanter people to be around. In this way, they make our social interactions go more smoothly.

A second question is how well the social intelligence model explains the workings of virtue in a corrupt or evil society. The social intelligence model has no difficulty with this. In general, social intelligence theory explains how and why virtue makes our lives go better by describing how and why virtue enables us to attain important goals of social living. This explanation can apply to reasonably just societies as well as to unjust or vicious societies, even though the latter constrict the virtuous person's options for social living. If career advancement, for example, is available only by swearing allegiance to a corrupt regime, the virtuous person's career will not advance, although non-virtuous forms of social intelligence could help the unscrupulous. If honesty in her interactions with others will result in the virtuous person's being turned in to the police by spies, the virtuous person's options for honest behavior are curtailed, and will need to be informed by prudence or practical wisdom. Such cases do not show that virtue is not social intelligence. What such cases do show is that some social goals cannot be achieved in evil circumstances unless one abandons virtue. Furthermore, these examples do not show that virtue is useless for achieving some social goals in evil times, nor that all social goals need be forfeited in corrupt circumstances. For example, having a harmonious family life, cultivating close personal friendships, and being just in one's business transactions could still be successfully pursued and achieved in corrupt social circumstances, and the attainment of these goals made possible by virtue as social intelligence.

6. CONCLUSION

The presentation of an empirically grounded theory of virtue is now complete. In chapter 1, I argued that virtues are subsets of CAPS traits, and pointed out that the existence of these traits is empirically supported. CAPS traits are manifested in behavior that is consistent across objectively different situation-types. Thus, the theory of CAPS traits addresses the concern of philosophical situationists that virtue theory lacks an empirically adequate moral psychology. In chapter 1, I also drew on the psychology of prejudice to sketch an empirically plausible model of deliberate virtue cultivation and vice inhibition. In chapter 2, I argued that goal-dependent automaticity provides an empirically adequate framework for understanding habitual virtuous actions. Habituation is, along with deliberate virtue cultivation, a way in which virtuous dispositions are formed. Chapters 3 and 4 used social intelligence theory to argue that virtue is a form of social intelligence, thereby providing a fresh perspective, also supported by empirical psychology, on how and why virtue helps us to live well—by providing us with the skills and abilities needed to successfully pursue social goals associated with valued life-tasks.

In chapter 5, I return to philosophical situationism. I reconsider the studies that philosophical situationists cite in favor of their views from the perspective of the virtue theory developed here. Key to this reconsideration is that these experiments raise explanatory puzzles that have prompted psychologists to look inward to the investigation of mental states to understand personality and behavior. This investigative path is one that does not preclude the existence of global traits.

5

PHILOSOPHICAL SITUATIONISM REVISITED

1. INTRODUCTION

Let us return to philosophical situationism. Harman (1999, 2000, 2003), Doris (1998, 2002, 2005), and Merritt (2000) cite studies in social psychology to argue that people generally act in response to features of situations and not on the basis of global traits. Harman believes these studies show that we have no empirical reason to think that global character traits exist (Harman 1999, 316; 2000, 223). He (1999, 316) writes: "It seems that ordinary attributions of character traits to people are often deeply misguided and it may even be the case that there is no such thing as character, no ordinary character traits of the sort people think there are, none of the usual moral virtues and vices." Doris (2002, 6) thinks the problem with character explanations is that "[t]hey presuppose the existence of character structures that actual people do not very often possess." Merritt (2000, 366) contends:

> The general thesis of situationism is that in reality, personal dispositions are highly situation-specific, with the consequence that we are in error to interpret behavioral consistencies in terms of robust traits. The preponderance of evidence drawn from systematic experimental observation, situationists say, supports the conclusion that individual behavior varies with situational variation in ways that familiar concepts of robust traits fail dismally to register.

Spelling out the implications of philosophical situationism for versions of virtue ethics that assume the existence of global traits, Harman (2000, 224) writes: "But if we know that there is no such thing as a character trait, and we know that virtue would require having character traits, there is nothing one can do to acquire character traits that are more like those possessed by a virtuous agent."

I hope by now to have convinced you that this bleak prognosis for virtue ethics is unwarranted. Empirical psychological studies show that personality is not necessarily fragmented, as philosophical situationists think. To the contrary, personality is coherent enough to warrant attributions of the kinds of traits that can be virtues. Let us reconsider the evidence philosophical situationists cite against the coherence of personality and behavioral manifestations of global traits in light of the picture of personality, character, and virtue developed in preceding chapters. A key theme in this reconsideration will be that situationist experiments leave us with puzzles regarding the explanation of how and why situations affect behavior. Psychologists recognize these puzzles, and seek to answer them by turning their focus inward to investigations of the mental states of agents, including the mechanisms by means of which subjects construe the situations with which they're presented. The situationist studies, I suggest, need not lead us down the path taken by Harman, Doris, and Merritt. Instead, puzzles raised by these experiments have led psychologists such as Mischel to investigate mechanisms of construal. When that path is taken, we can see the situationist experiments as parts of a larger psychological story that does not preclude global traits or virtues.

2. SOCIAL PSYCHOLOGY REVISITED

Philosophical situationists cite a wide array of social psychological studies to support their view that situations strongly influence behavior and that global traits have little to do with producing it. The main studies are: Hartshorne and May (1928), Newcomb (1929), Isen and Levin (1972), Darley and Batson (1973), studies of the effects of groups on helping behavior, the Stanford Prison Experiment (see Haney, Banks, and Zimbardo 1973; see also Zimbardo 2007), and Milgram (1974, 1977).

A. *Hartshorne and May (1928) and Newcomb (1929)*

Doris (2002, 24, 62–64) discusses Hartshorne and May's (1928) study of honest and deceptive behavior among eight thousand schoolchildren. According to the study, the children displayed inconsistently honest behavior, even across similar situations. Hartshorne and May (1928) concluded that honesty is not a trait or "inner entity," but a function of situational variables. According to Doris (2002, 24), Newcomb's (1929) study of introversion and extraversion in problem boys yielded similar results, finding that trait-relevant behaviors were not regular and consistent, but situation-sensitive. Doris (2002, 63) maintains that because the subjects were children, there are problems with regarding the studies as relevant to behavioral consistency in adults. He uses them only for the interpretative perspective they provide, and not for their evidentiary value.

Interestingly, Mischel (1968), too, was impressed by the Hartshorne and May studies. Yet the interpretative perspective he took was very different from Doris's. Mischel saw the Hartshorne and May results as evidence that the trait constructs then studied by personality psychology—global traits that were assumed to be manifested in behavior across many objectively different situation-types—were inadequate for explaining and predicting behavior. Instead of abandoning the search for behavioral consistency, however, Mischel looked for it in a different direction; he looked for it in response to situations as construed by the agent. Mischel, as well as other psychologists, for example, Ross and Nisbett (1991), appreciate the importance of construal in understanding personality functioning. Mischel and his collaborators have shown that, when situations are defined in terms of the meanings they have for agents, behavioral consistency across objectively different situation-types can be found.

B. Isen and Levin (1972) and Mood Effect Studies

Doris (2002, 30–32; 1998, 504) and Merritt (2000, 366, n. 2) also cite Isen and Levin (1972). Isen and Levin studied the effects of mood on helping behavior, and found that the only significant variable in whether subjects in a shopping mall stopped to help someone pick up papers dropped directly in their paths was whether they had just found a dime in the coin return slot of a phone booth. Isen and Levin's results are presented in Table 5.1.

They concluded that positive affect, understood as elevated mood or feeling good, induced in their study by situational factors, led to helping behavior. According to philosophical situationists, the relevance of Isen and Levin (1972) to global traits is this: if subjects had possessed global

Table 5.1

	Found Dime	Did Not Find Dime
Helped	14	1
Did Not Help	2	24

Table 5.2

	Found Dime	Did Not Find Dime
Helped	6	15
Did Not Help	9	20

traits such as compassion, surely they would have stopped to help even if they had not found a dime. In other words, trivial situational factors should not influence the exercise of virtue.

However, as Miller (2003, 389–392; see also Miller forthcoming) indicates and Doris (2002, 30, n. 4) acknowledges, researchers have had difficulty replicating the results of the Isen and Levin study. A similar experiment by Blevins and Murphy (1974) produced the results shown in Table 5.2. Blevins and Murphy did not find a correlation between finding a dime and helping.

In a manipulation of their original experiment, Levin and Isen (1975) gave subjects the opportunity to mail a stamped envelope apparently left behind in a phone booth. Subjects noticed the letter before checking the coin return slot. The results are shown in Table 5.3.

Weyant and Clark (1977) attempted to replicate Levin and Isen's (1975) findings. They report data from five different testing locations and over four times as many subjects as shown in Table 5.4. Weyant and Clark concluded that subjects who found a dime did not mail a letter more often than subjects who did not find a dime.

Given the difficulty of replicating their results, it is unclear how much support the Isen and Levin (1972) and Levin and Isen (1975) studies provide for the claim that situational influences lead to increased positive affect and helping behavior.[1]

However, as Miller (forthcoming) argues, mood effect studies, abundant in the social psychological literature, give more compelling support for the notion that situationally induced affect leads to helping behavior.[2]

Table 5.3

	Found Dime	Did Not Find Dime
Helped	10	1
Did Not Help	4	9

Table 5.4

	Found Dime	Did Not Find Dime
Helped	12	37
Did Not Help	15	42

A large trove of experiments indicate that apparently trivial factors, such as smelling pleasant fragrances in a shopping mall (Baron, 1997), or temperature (Anderson, Deuser, and DeNeve, 1995) affect helping behavior. In a careful review of this work, Miller (forthcoming), notes that both positive and negative affect can lead to increased helping behavior, and analyzes explanatory models offered in the psychological literature. He concludes that the implications of these studies for virtue ethics are mixed. I am skeptical that the studies are relevant for virtue ethics.

For one thing, many of the situations tested in the mood effect studies involve trivial forms of helping behavior, such as filling out surveys in shopping malls or giving change for a dollar. It is unclear which virtues would be implicated in these kinds of actions, so it is unclear which virtues would or would not be displayed in these experiments. Situations in which others are allegedly in serious need would provide better testing conditions for behavior expressing virtues such as compassion. A second point is that the results of the mood effect studies are compatible with small numbers of people possessing some virtue, or at least forms of civility. Since virtue ethicists acknowledge that virtuous people could be few and far between, the lack of helping behavior found in the absence of pleasant sensory stimuli need not be unsettling to the virtue ethicist. Finally, virtuous motives could be operative in addition to the motives produced by enhanced levels of the situationally induced affect that leads to helping behavior. Miller (forthcoming) recognizes these points, but argues that, on balance, the implications of the mood effect studies for virtue ethics are mixed. I think that more psychological work needs to be done testing affect and virtue before conclusions can clearly be drawn about the relevance of the mood effect studies for virtue ethics.

C. Darley and Batson (1973)

Let us turn now to Darley and Batson (1973), the famous study of Princeton seminarians, some of whom, in a hurry to get to a talk, stepped over a person slumped over and moaning, seemingly in need of help. In this experiment, cited by Doris (2002, 33–34; 1998, 510), Merritt (2000, 366, n. 2), and Harman (1999, 323–324), Princeton seminarians were recruited to participate in a study ostensibly on religious education and vocations. In the first part of the study, subjects completed questionnaires providing information on types of religiosity. In the second part, they reported to a building on campus ("Jerusalem") and were given a modest fee to give a talk at a site across campus ("Jericho"). When they reported to "Jerusalem," some seminarians were asked to speak about job prospects for seminary students; others were assigned the Parable of the

Good Samaritan. After being assigned their topics, subjects were placed in one of three "hurry conditions": high, intermediate, or low (Darley and Batson 1973, 103–104).

On the way from "Jerusalem" to "Jericho," subjects encountered a person slumped over and moaning, who, unbeknownst to them, was a confederate of the experimenters. Darley and Batson (1973, 104–105) report that of the 40 subjects, 16 (40%) offered some form of direct or indirect aid to the victim; 24 (60%) did not. By situational variable, percentages of subjects who offered aid were: for low hurry, 63% offered help; for intermediate hurry, 45%; and for high hurry, 10%. We should note that these results are consistent with small numbers of persons possessing compassion. Yet on several occasions, seminarians hurrying to speak about the parable of the Good Samaritan stepped over the slumped confederate on the way to give their talks (Darley and Batson 1973, 107). The researchers found that the only relevant variable in whether the subjects stopped to help was their degree of hurry. Type of religiosity as indicated on the questionnaires and the topic of the assigned talks were irrelevant to whether the seminarians stopped (Darley and Batson 1973, 107–108).

As Darley and Batson (1973, 107) note the overall picture painted by these findings is of a number of seminarians consciously noticing the person in distress and consciously choosing to leave him that way. Yet, they maintain that their post-experiment interviews with subjects suggest alternative interpretations. In the post-experiment interviews, all of the seminarians mentioned noticing the victim as possibly in need of help, but some did not consciously register this fact when they were near the victim. Darley and Batson (1973, 107–108) speculate that either the interpretation of their visual picture of someone in distress or their empathic reactions had been "deferred" because they were hurrying. As the researchers suggest, the mental states of those seminarians who did not consciously register the victim as needing help can be explained by saying that the "hurry" factor resulted in a "narrowing of the cognitive map." It is plausible to interpret the phrase, "narrowing of the cognitive map," to mean that, because of the "hurry" condition, the seminarians became overly focused on getting to their talks on time, and devoted diminished attentional resources to the victim's plight. A cognitive deficiency induced by the "hurry" condition, namely, misfocused attention, and not lack of compassion, could explain their failure to help.

My initial reaction to the "misfocused attention" explanation is that it is implausible to say that such a failure of attention is compatible with strongly possessing compassion. But the following counterargument might be made.[3] Becoming overly focused on a task often causes us to miss aspects of our surroundings. Thinking over my lecture on the way to class, for example, I completely miss the beautiful trees and sunshine. Absorbed as I am in hunting for an item on grocery stores shelves, a good friend must tap me on the shoulder to get my attention. Similarly, one might say, the focus on getting to their talks on time caused the seminarians to miss the plight of the "victim" in the Darley and Batson study. A lack of compassion is not their vice, but instead, their vice is a lack of attention or awareness or being too easily distracted. Lacking attention or awareness is different from lacking compassion. One might have the virtues, but be easily distracted or lack awareness. Lack of attention or awareness could be a general vice that affects all of the virtues, but not a limitation in any specific virtue.

If this line of reasoning is correct, one could say that the seminarians' vice is not a lack of compassion, but a general lack of awareness that caused them to be obtuse and miss a case relevant to virtue. This explanation parallels the account of Ian in the story of the dinner party mentioned in the last chapter. In this kind of case, one's general lack of awareness could be due to a lack of social intelligence. One simply is not keyed in to one's surrounding social milieu. So it is difficult to know whether those who failed to consciously register the "victim" lacked compassion or suffered from some other vice, such as general obtuseness.

Other seminarians apparently consciously decided not to stop, and appeared "aroused and anxious" after encountering the victim (Darley and Batson 1973, 108). The researchers suggest that for these seminarians, the conflict created by the need to offer help to the victim versus the commitment to "help" the interviewer by giving a talk could explain their leaving the victim. As Darley and Batson (1973, 108) remark, "Conflict, rather than callousness, can explain their failure to stop." Interestingly, Darley and Batson's final paragraph ends on a cautious note:

> Finally, as in other studies, personality variables were not useful in predicting whether a person helped or not. But in this study, unlike many previous ones, considerable variations were possible in the kinds of help given, and these variations did relate to personality measures—specifically to religiosity of the quest sort. The clear light of hindsight suggests that the dimension of kinds of helping would have been the appropriate place to look for personality differences all along; *whether* a person helps or not is an instant decision likely to be situationally controlled. How a person helps involves a more complex and considered number of decisions, including the time and scope to permit personality characteristics to shape them. (Darley and Batson 1973, 108, italics added)

Table 5.5

	Others Not Counting on Him Not Hurry	Others Not Counting on Him Hurry	Others Counting on Him Not Hurry	Others Counting on Him Hurry
Helped	8 of 10	7 of 10	5 of 10	1 of 10

Consider a follow-up study to Darley and Batson (1973) not usually cited by philosophical situationists. Batson et al. (1978) tested the hypothesis that hurry *per se* does not reduce helping behavior; instead, conflict over whom to help is the relevant factor. In this study, male undergraduates were told that their data either were or were not important for successful completion of a research project and were sent to another building to complete the project (Batson et al.1978, 97). Half were told that they were late and must hurry; the other half were told they had ample time. On their way, all encountered a male "victim," slumped over on the stairs, coughing and groaning. The results are shown in Table 5.5.

Batson et al. (1978, 100) contend: "Although the evidence is admittedly indirect, subjects' helping responses indicated that being in a hurry did not by itself reduce concern or compassion. For in one condition [others not counting on the subject] those in a hurry displayed considerable help." They maintain that conflict about whom to help—the "researcher" who needs data, or the "victim"—explains the behavior of those who failed to stop, not their callousness. Interestingly, Batson et al. (1978, 100) acknowledge the need to investigate the mental states of subjects, writing: "Ambiguity over the nature of the conflict suggests that we direct our future inquiry inward, to an analysis of the factors an individual considers in deciding whom to help. Does one consider the consequences for the people in need, for oneself, or both?"

In other words, that situations influence behavior is clear. To understand how situations affect behavior, and why individual differences in behavior occur among subjects under the same objective testing conditions, psychologists need to turn inward to the analysis of mental states. This move is similar to Mischel's recognition of the need to study subjects' construals of situations to understand their behavior and gain insights into personality functioning. As we saw in chapter 1, once subjects' construals are used in defining situations, the behavioral inconsistencies and apparent fragmentation of personality found in studies using situations defined solely in objective terms are minimized. Cross-situational behavioral consistency can be found sufficient to ground attributions of traits and warrant a more integrated picture of personality functioning.

Where does this discussion leave us with respect to Darley and Batson (1973), which is so often cited by philosophical situationists against the existence of character traits? I believe that study doesn't count against the existence of character traits, for the behavior of the seminarians could be explained in several ways that are compatible with the existence of virtues: the seminarians who stopped to help could have been motivated by compassion; those who did not register the presence of the "victim" and hurried on could have displayed either a lack of compassion or the vice of obtuseness to others; those who did notice the victim, hurried on, and showed anxiety afterwards could have experienced conflict about whom to help. None of these explanations disproves the existence of virtue, nor do they impugn my view of virtue as social intelligence.

D. Studies of the Effects of Groups on Helping Behavior

Doris (2002, 32–33) also discusses experiments testing the effects of groups on helping behavior. Widely replicated studies using a variety of experimental conditions show that lone subjects are more likely to come to the aid of others in apparent distress than when bystanders are present. In a useful review article, Latané and Nida (1981) analyze results from a large number of studies of the effects of groups on helping behavior. They tabulate data from fifty-seven experiments in which relatively high percentages of lone subjects came to the aid of perceived victims in simulated accidents such as crashes, explosions, falls, and fire alarms, as well as in simulated victimizations such as thefts (Latané and Nida 1981, 312–313). Percentages of lone subjects who helped in these experiments ranged from 47% to 100%. When confederates of the experimenters or others were present, the percentages of subjects who helped ranged from 5% to 100%.

Studies of the effects of groups on helping behavior document conditions under which psychologists interpret the presence of bystanders as *inhibiting* helping behavior (Latané and Nida 1981, 308). Psychologists conclude that helping behavior is *inhibited* by the presence of groups—and not simply that it is absent—by contrasting the lack of helping behavior in the presence of groups with another robust experimental finding, namely, that lone individuals consistently come to the aid of others perceived to be in distress. If helping behavior is assumed to be produced by a trait, then, in keeping with situationist interpretations, aggregating these data would seem to provide some evidence of strong possession of a trait that could be considered a virtue—compassion or benevolence. But if so, then, taken together, the studies of helping behavior, both of lone individuals and of subjects in the presence of groups, do not show either that there is no empirical reason to believe that character traits exist or that traits likely to be virtues have little to do with producing behavior. Instead, they document conditions under which virtue-relevant behavior is likely to be expressed—when lone individuals are confronted with persons perceived to be in distress—as well as when such behavior is likely to be inhibited—when individuals are confronted with similar scenarios in the presence of groups.

It is natural to ask why helping behavior is inhibited in the group testing conditions. Psychologists adduce several different mechanisms to explain the inhibiting effects of the presence of others on helping behavior: audience inhibition, according to which a subject's helping behavior is inhibited by the fear of embarrassment at the prospect of misinterpreting a situation as an emergency; social influence, according to which helping behavior is inhibited when a subject looks to the reactions of others for cues as to how a situation should be interpreted; and diffusion of responsibility, according to which the costs of nonintervention are shared among others who are present (see Latané and Nida 1981, 309; Doris 2002, 32–33; for a general discussion of the effects of groups on helping behavior, see Latané and Darley 1970). Interestingly, each of these mechanisms purports to give some insight into the mental state of the agent whose behavioral expression of helping is checked. Each offers a theory of how subjects construe situations to explain the lack of helping behavior. Proponents of audience inhibition, for example, explain subjects' lack of behavior by positing that they fear being mistaken about the situation and acting foolishly in the eyes of the others present. The social influence account hypothesizes that the subject is unsure of her own perception of the situation, and looks to the reactions of others for cues to guide her own construal of events—again, a commentary on the subject's mental state. Finally, those who posit diffusion of responsibility attribute to subjects a cost-benefit calculation of whether to act in the circumstances—a conjecture about what is going on in their minds that deters them from helping.

Remarking on these mechanisms, Doris (2002, 33) maintains: "The operative processes are doubtless complicated, but one general implication of the group effect studies seems fairly clear: Mild social pressures can result in neglect of apparently serious ethical demands." Doris is surely right to observe that, in the group effect experiments, mild social pressures resulted in the lack of helping behavior. If the foregoing explanations are correct, mild social pressures do this via their effect on how the agents construe the situations. Data on helping behavior are thus an invitation to further psychological study of how subjects' construals of situations influence their behavior. This reflects the theme emerging in our discussion of situationist experiments: these studies create puzzles about the explanation of behavior. Even if they show that situations influence behavior, they cry out for further explanation of how situations have the effects they do, and of why some subjects behave differently from others in the same objective testing conditions. A second emerging theme is that psychologists recognize these questions, and seek to answer them by focusing on the investigation of agents' mental states, including mechanisms of construal. That is, the response of psychologists to situationist experiments differs from Doris's. Doris claims that the experiments cited by philosophical situationists, taken together, document narrow behavioral regularities that are specific to situations defined in purely objective terms. He posits local traits, such as "office party sociability," to explain these regularities, but seems to recognize that this is an unpromising explanatory strategy (see Doris 2002, 66). To the best of my knowledge, no psychologists make the same move—recall that CAPS traits, even if local, are indexed to the meanings situations have for subjects. More than Doris, psychologists focus on agents' powers of construal to explain the puzzles raised by situationist experiments.

E. The Stanford Prison Experiment (1971)

The Stanford prison experiment (Haney, Banks, and Zimbardo 1973; Haney and Zimbardo 1977; Haney and Zimbardo 1998; see also Zimbardo 2007) is also cited by Doris (2002, 51–53; see also 1998, 526, nn. 48 and 49) as evidence of the power of situational influences on behavior. In August of 1971, psychologist Philip Zimbardo and his colleagues set up a simulated prison using Stanford University students (Zimbardo 2007, xv). Eighteen subjects were randomly assigned the roles of "prisoners" and "guards." The experiment, originally scheduled for two weeks, had to be discontinued after a few days as the "guards" became too involved in their roles and engaged in brutal and degrading behavior toward the "prisoners," such as forcing them to clean toilets with their bare hands and attempting to force feed them (Haney and Zimbardo 1998, 709; Doris 2002, 51; Zimbardo 2007). Doris (2002, 52–53) concludes that the situational pressures of the simulated prison conditions, and not traits possessed by subjects, accounted for their behavior during the experiment. In an article reflecting on the twenty-fifth anniversary of the Stanford Prison Experiment, the organizers of the experiment apparently agree, citing "… the power of social situations to overwhelm individual dispositions and even to degrade the quality of human nature" (Zimbardo, Maslach, and Haney 2000, 193–194). According to them, the simulated conditions of the Stanford Prison Experiment created a "total situation" in which "… the processes of deindividuation and dehumanization are institutionalized" (Zimbardo, Maslach, and Haney 2000, 193). A total situation is one in which some people, such as prisoners of war, are under the complete control of others.

I believe the Stanford Prison Experiment should be approached with care. For one thing, students were recruited for a psychological experiment in which they knew they would be simulating a prison, and in which some were expected to play the roles of guards and some, prisoners. Mightn't they be disposed to role-play as part of the experiment? That is, mightn't they be disposed to put their natural reactions "on hold" and "play along" for the sake of the experiment? For another, at least one "prisoner" complained about bad treatment from the guards and a violation of the contract between the experimenters and the subjects. Zimbardo convinced him to stay on, earn his money, which would be forfeited if he quit early, and receive special treatment in exchange for "snitching" on fellow "prisoners" (see Zimbardo 2007, 68–69). This "prisoner" led others to believe that their contracts with Zimbardo couldn't be broken (see Zimbardo 2007, 70–71). Commenting on this stage of the experiment, Zimbardo (2007, 71) writes: "Nothing could have had a more transformative impact on the prisoners than the sudden news that in this experiment they had lost their liberty to quit on demand, lost their power to walk out at will. At that moment, the Stanford Prison Experiment was changed into the Stanford Prison, not by any top-down formal declarations by the staff but by this bottom-up declaration from one of the prisoners themselves."

I think the experiment was changed into "Stanford Prison," if it was, by the manipulation of the subjects' construals of the situation. To me, the Stanford Prison Experiment shows that college-aged students' perceptions and behavior can be manipulated. We know from history that total situations can overwhelm individual dispositions and cause persons to treat their fellows in degrading and inhumane ways; we did not need the Stanford Prison Experiment to tell us that. To my mind, the Stanford Prison Experiment tells us very little about how and why personality and behavior are disrupted by pervasive situational influences. To understand how apparently ordinary people can perpetrate abuses against others under certain circumstances, we need to look to other experimental work. Light is shed on the conditions under which guards, for example, are able to abuse prisoners by social-cognitivist psychologist Albert Bandura (1998, 1999, 2004). Bandura examines mechanisms of moral disengagement that blunt the internalized self-sanctions, such as moral codes, empathy with victims, or a guilty conscience, that might otherwise curtail aggression (see Bandura 1998, 180–181; Bandura 1999; Bandura, Barbaranelli, Caprara, and Pastorelli 1996). Such mechanisms of disengagement focus on how reprehensible conduct, detrimental effects, and victims are portrayed in the minds of perpetrators (see Bandura 1998, 162;

Bandura 2004, 123). Without going into detail about Bandura's work, we should note that he has studied the mechanisms of construal that enable perpetrators to view victims as less than fully human, or see their own actions as in the service of a just cause, or shunt responsibility for what they do onto others. Once again, a focus on how people construe situations is key to understanding personality functioning and behavior, including people's responses to the situational forces that affect them.

One final point apropos the Stanford Prison Experiment is worth calling to mind. Total situations do not always overwhelm individual dispositions. Admiral James B. Stockdale survived seven and a half years as a prisoner of war in Vietnam (see Sherman 2005, 1–7). He had read and internalized Epictetus's *Enchiridion*, a source which helped bolster him (presumably his character) in the face of adversity. Furthermore, in her acceptance speech for the Republican Party's nomination for vice president in September, 2008, Governor Sarah Palin praised presidential nominee Senator John McCain's courage under similar circumstances. Neither Doris nor Zimbardo would deny that such courage exists, nor that individual dispositions can withstand and counter situational forces. It is uninformative simply to say, however, either that situations can overwhelm dispositions or that dispositions can withstand situations. We need to know more about how the interaction of situational and dispositional factors occurs. To belabor a by-now familiar theme, many psychologists have recognized that understanding personality and behavior requires that we look to the roles construal plays in explaining how situations affect dispositions, and vice versa. Investigating the mental states of agents and how they perceive the situational forces that affect them is how progress in understanding personality and behavior has been made.

F. Milgram's Obedience Experiments

Doris (2002, 39–51; 1998, 510, 516–517; see also Harman 1999, 321–323) devotes extensive commentary to the famous Milgram (1974, 1977) obedience studies.[4] Widely replicated in a number of countries and using a variety of investigational manipulations, the studies asked people from various walks of life to participate in an "experiment." The ostensible purpose was to test the effects of punishment on memory. Subjects, designated "teachers," were asked to administer a series of increasingly severe shocks of up to 450 volts to "learners," who, unbeknown to subjects, were confederates of the experimenters. In fact, the shocks were dummy shocks. The real point of the Milgram studies was to test attitudes toward authority. As Milgram puts it, the specific question under investigation was: "If an experimenter tells a subject to hurt another person, under what conditions will the subject go along with this instruction, and under what conditions will he refuse to obey" (Milgram 1977, 102).

In Milgram's original experiments, several manipulations of experimental conditions were used, and forty fresh adult subjects were studied in each condition (Milgram 1977, 103, 106). One series of such manipulations tested the effects of the physical proximity of "learners" on subjects' behavior. In the first of these conditions, called "remote feedback," subjects sat in front of a simulated control panel, while "learners" were taken into an adjacent room and were strapped into a simulated electric chair. Subjects were instructed to switch a lever on the panel to administer a shock to the "learner" when he or she got a wrong answer. The simulated shock generator automatically recorded the voltage levels that subjects gave. At the 300 volt level, the "learner" pounded on the wall; at 315 volts he was no longer heard from. The second condition in the series, called "voice feedback," was identical to the first except that the complaints of the "learner" in the adjacent room were audible through a door left slightly ajar and through the walls of the laboratory. In the third experimental condition, called "proximity," subjects were placed in the same room with the "learners," who were visible as well as audible. The fourth manipulation in the series, "touch-proximity," was identical to the third, except that the "learner" received a shock only when his hand rested on a shockplate. At 150 volts, the "learner" demanded to be released from the experiment, and refused to put his hand on the plate. The experimenter ordered the subject to force the "learner's" hand onto the plate. "Obedient" subjects were defined as those who followed instructions to shock all the way to the maximum level of 450 volts; "defiant" subjects were defined as those who disobeyed or defied instructions at some point. Results are shown in Table 5.6.

Another set of manipulations varied the physical proximity and degree of surveillance of the experimenter (Milgram 1977, 110). Three conditions were studied: one in which the experimenter sat a few feet away from the subject; one in which the experimenter left the laboratory and issued instructions by telephone; and one in which the experimenter was never seen, but gave instructions by a tape recording that was activated when subjects entered the laboratory. Milgram (1977, 110) writes: "Obedi-

Table 5.6

	Remote Condition	**Voice Feedback Condition**	**Proximity Condition**	**Touch-Proximity Condition**
% of subjects who defied experimenter	34%	37.5%	60%	70%

ence dropped sharply as the experimenter was physically removed from the laboratory. The number of obedient subjects in the first condition (Experimenter Present) was almost three times as great as in the second, where the experimenter gave his orders by telephone. Twenty-six subjects were fully obedient in the first condition, and only nine in the second ..." Milgram (1977, 110) also reports that when the experimenter was absent, several subjects gave lower shocks than required but did not inform the experimenter; additionally, some subjects reported to the experimenter by telephone that they were raising the level of shocks according to instructions, all the while repeatedly giving the lowest level of shocks on the board.

Further variations also yielded interesting results. When two experimenters gave conflicting instructions, one telling subjects to continue, the other telling them to stop, all of the subjects stopped (Sabini and Silver 2005, 551). Similarly, when two peer subjects taking part in the experiment refused to continue, ninety percent of the subjects followed suit (Milgram 1977, 117; Sabini and Silver 2005, 551, n. 41). In a variation in which no authority was ordering escalation, some subjects forcibly came to the victim's aid (Sabini and Silver 2005, 553, n. 44). A variation manipulating institutional context was also performed: experiments were moved from Yale University, with its aura of prestige and authority, to a bland office building in nearby Bridgeport, Connecticut. Milgram (1977, 116) reports that obedience levels were not significantly lower among Bridgeport subjects than among their Yale counterparts: "... 48 percent of the Bridgeport subjects delivered the maximum shock versus 65 percent in the corresponding condition at Yale."

Interestingly, Milgram (1977, 119) writes that his experiments are not "... directed toward an exploration of the motives engaged when the subject obeys the experimenter's commands. Instead, they examine the situational variables responsible for the elicitation of obedience." Yet the results are troubling, and they raise questions. Under some conditions, subjects forcibly aided the victim. Under some, they openly disobeyed the order to shock. Under others, they surreptitiously disobeyed and lied about it to the experimenter. Under still other conditions, subjects obeyed but showed signs of tension and anxiety. Milgram (1974, 44) analyzes post-experiment interviews with subjects in an effort to better understand the obedience studies, claiming:

> From each person in the experiment we derive one essential fact: whether he has obeyed or disobeyed. But it is foolish to see the subject only in this way. For he brings to the laboratory a full range of emotions, attitudes, and individual styles. Indeed, so varied

> in temperament and manner are the people passing through the laboratory that it sometimes seems a miracle that we emerge with any regularities at all....
>
> We need to focus on the individuals who took part in the study not only because this provides a personal dimension to the experiment but also because the quality of each person's experience gives us clues to the nature of the process of obedience.

Toward the end of his book, Milgram (1974, 205) writes: "I am certain that there is a complex personality basis to obedience and disobedience. But I know we have not found it."

The complexity of subjects' behavior under varying experimental conditions testifies to the effects of the situation in influencing behavior, but does not answer questions about the role of personality variables. However, the data belie either the conclusion that subjects did not possess traits, or that they possessed traits, but not strongly enough for the traits to influence their behavior. In an extensive review of obedience studies, Blass (1991) maintains that some personality measures can predict obedience, and that enduring beliefs, another kind of dispositional variable, are also implicated in obedience.[5] He notes that the first published study (Elms and Milgram, 1966; see also Elms, 1972) that examined the relationship between personality and obedience in the Milgram experiments found obedients to rate significantly higher on authoritarianism than disobedients (Blass 1991, 402). This study also found a correlation between defiant subjects from Milgram's experiments and their scores on a social responsibility scale (see Blass 1991, 402); two other studies also found correlations between obedience and authoritarianism in subjects (see Blass 1991, 402–403). Haas (1966), a separate study of obedience also discussed by Blass (1991, 403), asked lower-level company managers to evaluate their superiors and indicate whom they felt should be fired. Their recommendations were to serve as "the final basis for action" (quoted in Blass 1991, 403). Blass (1991, 403) reports: "Haas (1966) found a significant positive correlation ... between the managers' degree of obedience and their hostility ..." According to the studies discussed by Blass, authoritarianism and hostility correlate positively with obedient behavior, whereas social responsibility (which we might not want to call a 'trait') correlates with disobedient behavior.

In a review of other studies on obedience to authority, Blass (1991, 405) found that beliefs about external controlling influences on one's life affect obedience: "... beliefs about ceding versus retaining personal control seem to be salient and predisposing factors in obedience to authority. The evidence, in this regard, is clearest with religious variables, that is variables centered around the belief that one's life is under divine control...." High scorers on personality scales measuring religious beliefs tended to be more obedient than low scorers or those who rejected any authority.

Blass (1991, 408) is quite measured about the conclusions to be drawn from his review of obedience studies, contending:

> My review has shown that although amount of obedience can vary as a function of situational manipulations and differ among individuals within the same setting, neither the proposed situational dimensions (e. g., immediacy or salience of victim) nor the personality variables studied as potential individual-difference correlates (e. g., authoritarianism) have accounted for the variations in a consistent, orderly, and predictable manner. Situational and personality perspectives on the obedience findings are on equal footing because their problem is essentially the same: discovering the constructs that can account for variations in obedience in a coherent way.

Sabini and Silver (2005, 560, n. 56) go further than Blass. Citing Blass (1991) as well as Elms and Milgram (1966), they argue:

> ... in the Milgram experiment authoritarianism does predict behavior.... And, indeed, it has been argued that personality variables predict obedience better than do situational variables. But beyond that, we have suggested that in all of these experiments [experiments on social influence, such as Darley and Batson (1973), Milgram's experiments, and studies of the effects of groups on helping behavior] subjects want to, are inclined to, are disposed to do the right thing, but they are inhibited.

Sabini and Silver (2005, 560) believe that people "... lose their moral compass" and that this weakness is partly cognitive, but is partly a matter of being unwilling or afraid to expose their perceptions to the world.

What should we conclude from this lengthy discussion of Milgram? For one thing, the interpretation of the results of Milgram's experiments is still a matter of controversy. Psychologists, including Milgram himself, have looked for a basis in personality variables to explain the results. Evidence that personality factors are involved in obedience to authority has been interpreted with more or less caution by those who are familiar with the relevant studies. Blass (1991), who is cautious, recognizes that more work needs to be done to elucidate both the situational and the personality factors that can coherently account for variations in obedience. Sabini and Silver (2005), who are more speculative, identify perceptions and construal as important factors in understanding both people's behavior in the Milgram studies and the behavior in other studies of social influences that are cited by philosophical situationists. So our treatment of Milgram ends on a familiar note: the Milgram experiments, like other studies that philosophical situationists cite, raise more questions than they answer, crying out for further analysis and clarification of results.

3. CONCLUSION

We can agree with philosophical situationists that most of the studies reviewed in this chapter attest to the power of situations in influencing behavior. What do they imply about virtue and character, as traditionally conceived? A number of philosophers have argued that the studies tell us little, if anything, about the role of virtue in producing behavior, nor do they give us reason to abandon traditional notions of virtue and character (see, for example, Kupperman 2001; Sreenivasan 2002; Miller 2003; Montmarquet 2003; Kamtekar 2004; Sabini and Silver 2005; Webber 2006a, 2006b, 2007; and Wielenberg 2006). I agree; however, my take on the implications of the situationist studies for virtue ethics places them in the context of a larger psychological story.

Key to this bigger picture is a lesson that emerges from most of the studies. It is encapsulated in the approaches of Darley and Batson (1973), Milgram (1974), and those who posit psychological mechanisms to better understand why groups inhibit helping behavior: the behavioral findings of the studies situationists cite need to be supplemented with investigations into the mental states of the subjects if these experiments are to be useful tools for understanding human behavior. The clear message of this approach, as Mischel realized, is that situations have meanings for people. To understand subjects' behavior in experimental circumstances, we need to understand how they understand the situation. This takes us beyond the social psychological experiments philosophical situationists cite, as well as beyond their interpretations of those experiments.

We should read the situationist experiments as stepping stones on the path of personality science. They were a challenge to trait theories that prevailed in the late 1960s and 1970s. They prompted further experimental work and a reconceptualization of traits and personality by Mischel and Shoda. This trait reconceptualization is good news for virtue ethics. In addition to other empirical work, Mischel and Shoda's (1995) CAPS traits provide the traditional notion of virtue with firm grounding in empirical psychology. In the conclusion to this volume, I revisit the journey taken thus far, and indicate areas for further exploration.

CONCLUSION

The purpose of this book has been to articulate and defend an empirically grounded theory of virtue. My approach has been ecumenical, relying on a conception of virtue that is common to several versions of virtue ethics. This conception of virtue is familiar to philosophers: virtues are enduring character traits incorporating practical reason, appropriate motivation, and affect, and manifested in cross-situationally consistent behavior. My aim has been to respond to the skepticism of philosophical situationists, who believe that such a notion of virtue is not adequately grounded in empirical psychology. I hope to have shown their skepticism to be misplaced.

The journey we have made has taken us into the territories of philosophy and psychology. Like the philosophical situationists, I believe that philosophers have much to learn from studying the work of psychologists. Unlike them, however, I find that empirical psychology does not threaten, but instead, sustains the conception of virtues as global traits. Only a very narrow reading of the situation-trait debate between social psychologists and personality theorists, I believe, supports the philosophical situationist position. This debate, when seen as a snapshot or time slice of a longer debate that spans the 20th and 21st centuries, yields a more positive perspective on global traits and the unified, coherent conception of personality which the notion of global traits implies.

The work of Walter Mischel and Yuichi Shoda (1999) on the CAPS conception of personality is central to this outlook. As they and other psychologists recognize, the social psychological experiments on which philosophical situationists rely looked at the wrong kinds of situations to test for behavioral manifestations of traits. Behavioral consistency across objectively different situation-types was found when situations were defined in terms of the meanings they had for subjects. Such behavioral consistency warrants attributions of traits with the potential to be global. Virtues can plausibly be considered a subset of these traits. Virtue ethics, then, should not be unsettled by the claims of philosophical situationism.

The story does not end with empirical evidence of the existence of traits that can be virtues. The development of virtue through both deliberate cultivation and habitual virtuous action can be explicated using empirical psychology. Studies in the psychology of prejudice show how character can be shaped through the inhibition and control of stereotype activation. This model is promising for understanding deliberate virtue cultivation and vice inhibition. Moreover, habitual virtuous action can be understood and its rationality defended using empirical research on goal-dependent automaticity. Finally, social intelligence theory can be used to explain how and why having the virtues makes our lives go better. Social intelligence is social savvy—the cognitive and affective knowledge, skills, and sensitivities needed to deal with people and effectively navigate social life. Virtues, I've argued, are forms of social intelligence that enable us to understand and act well in social interactions and advance virtue-relevant goals. The upshot of all this is that various research traditions in empirical psychology furnish valuable windows on a familiar topic—what virtues are, how they can be cultivated, and how they can improve our lives.

The work done in this book is a beginning. Much remains to be done in developing virtue theory, especially at the interfaces between virtue and psychology. The implications of mood effect studies for virtue ethics and other ethical theory-types is one promising area for future development (see Miller, forthcoming). Psychological studies of self-regulation and self-determination, too, will likely interest those concerned with virtue ethics and virtue theory (see Besser-Jones 2008). Finally, empirical studies of happiness should be relevant to eudaimonistic virtue ethics (see Snow 2008). As I said in the introduction to this volume, virtue ethics is alive and well. May it continue.

NOTES

INTRODUCTION

1. For the distinction between virtue ethics and virtue theory, see Hursthouse (2007).
2. Campbell (1999) also refers to social psychological studies, but explores their implications for philosophical accounts of altruism. For earlier philosophical discussions of the social psychological studies philosophical situationists cite, see Kupperman (1991) and Flanagan (1991). For explanations of situationism in psychology, see Mischel (1968), Krahé (1990), and Ross and Nisbett (1991).
3. Merritt (2000) uses local traits to argue that virtue can be socially sustained through the construction of suitable social environments. Doris (2002, 90–91) is skeptical of this project, in part because of the difficulties of knowing what the social environments are that are conducive to the virtues we want, as well as of constructing such environments.

CHAPTER 1

1. See, for example, Andersen, Thorpe, and Kooij (2007), Funder (2006), Funder (2001), Kenrick and Funder (1988).
2. This view of how personality shapes construals of situations is similar to that expressed by Kamtekar (2004, 471), when she asks, "... why is how we construe our situations not part of our character?"
3. For other empirical studies, see Vansteelandt and Van Mechelen (1998), Andersen and Chen (2002), Borkenau, Riemann, Spinath, and Angleitner (2006), Cervone and Shoda (1999), and Shoda and LeeTiernan (2002).
4. The mean frequencies of encountering each type of situation, with standard deviation in parentheses, were: Peer teased, provoked, or threatened, 10.3 (6.5); Adult warned the child, 42.9 (19.5); Adult gave the child time out, 22.8 (16.0); Peer initiated positive social contact, 39.8 (10.5); Adult praised the child verbally, 66.5 (14.6) (Shoda, Mischel, and Wright 1994, 677).
5. I owe this point to Jason Kawall.

6. I am grateful to Christian Miller for this objection as well as for providing numerous references to the mood effect studies. Jason Kawall also brought the mood effect studies to my attention, and they are mentioned by Doris (2002, 28).
7. See the studies by Mischel, Shoda, and Wright referenced earlier in the text, as well as those listed in note 3.
8. For the complexities involved in identifying "traditional moral trait taxonomies," see John and Srivastava (1999), 102–138. For a perspective similar to mine on the relevance of CAPS traits to situationism and virtue ethics, see Miller (2003), 382–388. See also Adams (2006), 131–132 on the relevance of Mischel's work to the situationist debate.
9. See Lord (1982) for more information about each of these methods.
10. This example highlights a problem that arises in attempts to infer traits from behavioral measures alone: there is no guarantee of a one-to-one correspondence between behavior and trait. We cannot infer directly from one kind of behavior to the same kind of trait; e.g., someone may behave quietly in church because she is respectful of others, because she is afraid to draw attention to herself, because she is a conformist, etc., not because she is a quiet person. See Sabini and Silver (2005), 540–544; Kamtekar (2004), 474; Sreenivasan (2002), 50–51; and McCrae and Costa (1996), 74.
11. I thank Stephen Franzoi for pointing out to me that our ability to shape our personalities is limited.
12. I am indebted to Stephen Franzoi for alerting me to the work of Devine and Monteith.

CHAPTER 2

1. Bargh (1989, 3) claims that automatic actions are not consumptive of the limited processing capacity of the agent; at Bargh (1989, 5), he claims that ". . . they will operate even when attentional resources are scarce." Since it makes more sense to think that automatic processes consume some processing capacity, I rely on the claim made at Bargh (1989, 5).
2. If I am unaware that a stimulus has activated a stereotype that is influencing my action, I cannot *immediately* deliberately intervene to counter its effects. However, if, after a while, I realize that the stereotype has been triggered and is having an impact, surely then I can intervene to counter it.
3. Strictly speaking, the representation of the goal, and not the goal itself, is nonconsciously activated. I try to be as precise as possible, and refer mainly to the activated representation of the goal. Sometimes this locution is cumbersome, and I refer simply to the activation of the goal. One might think that referring to the representation of a goal, as opposed to simply referring to a goal, is to introduce a distinction without a difference, since having a goal is the same thing as having a representation of it. This is not quite right, however, for my representation can extend beyond the conceptual content of the goal itself. We can see this by noting that representations of goals can change, yet the goal itself remains the same. My goal to lose weight, for example, can remain essentially the same in terms of conceptual content, yet my representation of it can change from negative to positive, depending on changes in the attitude with which I view it.
4. For consequentially ascribable versus independently intelligible desires, on which I draw for insight about goal ascription, see Dancy (1993, 8-9).
5. I owe this example to Timothy Crockett.
6. Such virtue ethicists include Aristotle (1985), McDowell (1995), Zagzebski (1996), Hursthouse (1999), Foot (2001), Slote (2001), and Swanton (2003). One should recall here the distinction between virtue ethics and virtue theory noted in the introduction to this volume. Virtue theory is an area of moral psychology that provides an account of what virtue is. Virtue theories can be developed in conjunction with normative ethical

theories such as consequentialism and deontology. By contrast, virtue ethics is a type of normative ethical theory that takes virtue as its central concept, and provides a fully-blown theoretical alternative to consequentialism and deontology. Virtue ethics includes, but is not limited to, virtue theory. Some virtue theorists, e.g., Driver (2001), disagree that virtuous motivations are required for truly virtuous actions. But it is unclear that these virtue theorists are describing virtue in a recognizable sense. Driver's theory of virtue, as I argued in the introduction, is untenable.

7. The analogy of virtue-relevant goals with deep language structures can be taken only so far. My claim is not that representations of virtue-relevant goals are innate, as are language capacities, only that they are deep-seated.

CHAPTER 3

1. Cognitive ethologists have also studied social intelligence. Byrne and Whiten (1988), Byrne (1995), and Whiten and Byrne (1997) advance the Machiavellian Intelligence hypothesis, according to which human cognitive evolution is driven by social intelligence. According to this hypothesis, biological fitness was obtained by those of our ancestors who were able to represent to themselves the beliefs, desires, and motives of others, and thereby could know who was likely to cooperate with them and who was likely to cheat and deceive. For discussion, see Sterelny (1998, 26) and Holekamp (2007, 65–9). The Machiavellian Intelligence hypothesis, though interesting, is here left aside.
2. Studies by Bruner, Shapiro, and Tagiuri (1958) and Cantor (1978) found many social characteristics among people's lists of what they thought were attributes of intelligent people. Sternberg, Conway, Ketron, and Bernstein (1981) found such attributes as "accepts others for what they are," "admits mistakes," "displays interest in the world at large," "is on time for appointments," and "has social conscience" to be prototypical of people's conceptions of social intelligence. Ford and Miura (1983), Kozmitzki and John (1993), and Schneider, Ackerman, and Kanfer (1996) have unearthed similar prototypical features of people's conceptions of social intelligence.
3. For discussion, see Kihlstrom and Cantor (2000, 363); Jones and Day (1997, 487); Wong, Day, Maxwell, and Meara (1995, 117). For earlier attempts at measurement and a general summary of empirical work on social intelligence, see Kihlstrom and Cantor (2000, 359–363); Wong, Day, Maxwell, and Meara (1995, 117); and Sternberg and Smith (1985, 169–173).
4. See, for example, Marlowe and Bedell (1982), Frederickson, Carlson, and Ward (1984), Marlowe (1986), Lowman and Leeman (1988), Barnes and Sternberg (1989), Brown and Anthony (1990), Stricker and Rock (1990), Riggio, Messamer, and Throckmorton (1991), Legree (1995), Wong, Day, Maxwell, and Meara (1995), and Jones and Day (1997).
5. In the working definition of social intelligence used here and in subsequent formulations, I understand the term "knowledge' to include social memory, that is, the ability to store social information in short- and long-term memory and to recall it when appropriate.
6. Baron-Cohen et al. 1999 furnish evidence that different brain areas are active when normal subjects and patients with autism or Asberger syndrome perform social intelligence tests.
7. Studies have shown that people lacking in empathic sensitivity, such as high-functioning autistics and those with Asberger syndrome, are also lacking in social intelligence (see Baron-Cohen et al. 1999, 1891).
8. Here is one important dissimilarity between the two approaches. The perspective presented by social intelligence enables us to have greater facility in attaining our social goals; the vantage point afforded by Buddhism enables us to see that our social goals might not be as important as we had thought.

CHAPTER 4

1. McDowell's view of the unitary motivational state of virtuous agents is susceptible of different interpretations: the unitary state could be interpreted as beliefs that motivate, or as "besires," that is, unitary states with opposite directions of fit.
2. Contrary to the position stated in the text, one might be inclined to claim that it is intelligible for someone to desire to help another without genuinely believing the other needs help. Someone might desire to help another, and, motivated by her desire, fabricate the false and self-deceptive belief that she needs help. This would explain how it could be intelligible for someone to desire to help another, yet not truly believe the other needs help. In this case, I would deny that the desire to help the other is either genuine or her true motivating factor. What is more likely in this case is that we are presented with a complex motivational state in which one person really desires to control another, or for some other reason, perhaps in order to ingratiate herself for personal gain, desires to be of help to another whom she knows neither needs nor wants her help. The one with the alleged desire to help convinces herself that she desires to help the other out of simple good will or benevolence, and manufactures the false and self-deceptive belief that the other genuinely needs help to avoid confronting her true desires. Throughout the text, I assume that the surface desires of an individual, such as her desire to help another, are the true motivating factors operative in her psyche. As Nietzsche and depth psychologists recognize, however, this assumption need not be true. Depth psychology contends that many motivating factors can be operative at deeper levels of consciousness. The motivational complexities presented by depth psychology are here left aside.

CHAPTER 5

1. See also Miller (forthcoming), cited by permission of the author.
2. Miller (forthcoming) cites: Baron (1997), Anderson, Deuser, and DeNeve (1995), Cunningham (1979), Mathews and Canon (1975), Berg (1978), Rosenhan, Salovey, and Hargis (1981), Donnerstein, Donnerstein, and Munger (1975), Gifford (1988), and overviews: Carlson, Charlin, and Miller (1988) and Schaller and Cialdini (1990).
3. I owe this argument to Jason Kawall.
4. See also Zimbardo (2007, 266ff) for interesting discussion of Milgram's experiments and similar experimental models.
5. As an interesting note, a study by Burley and McGuinness (1977) found that subjects who did not comply with the experimenter's orders to administer shocks to "learners" in a Milgram-type experiment scored significantly higher on a social intelligence test than those who did comply:

   > The subjects of low social intelligence showed both in the experiment and in the interviews that they were dependent on the experimenter's judgment and held him responsible, while the subjects of high social intelligence but disobedient had appeared to view the situation objectively and had acted on the basis of their own judgment. (Burley and McGuinness 1977, 769–770)

   Blass (1991, 403) cautions, however, that the study was performed using only twenty-four subjects, and social intelligence was tested using an instrument, dating from 1927, that was unlikely to be up to contemporary psychometric standards.

REFERENCES

Aars, H. and A Dijksterhuis. 2000. Habits as Knowledge Structures: Automaticity in Goal-Directed Behavior. *Journal of Personality and Social Psychology* 78: 53–63.

Adams, R. M. 2006. *A Theory of Virtue: Excellence in Being for the Good.* New York: Oxford University Press.

Andersen, S. M., and S. Chen. 2002. The Relational Self: An Interpersonal Social-Cognitive Theory. *Psychological Review* 109(4): 619–645.

Andersen, S. M., J. S. Thorpe, and C. S. Kooij. 2007. Character in Context: The Relational Self and Transference. In *Persons in Context: Building a Science of the Individual.* Eds. Y. Shoda, D. Cervone, and G. Downey. New York: Guilford, 169–200.

Anderson, C., W. Deuser, and K. DeNeve 1995. Hot Temperatures, Hostile Affect, Hostile Cognition, and Arousal: Tests of a General Model of Affective Aggressiveness. *Personality and Social Psychology Bulletin* 21: 434–448.

Annas, J. 2005. Comments on John Doris's *Lack of Character. Philosophy and Phenomenological Research* LXXI(3): 636-642.

Aristotle. 1985. *Nicomachean Ethics.* Trans. T. Irwin. Indianapolis, IN: Hackett Publishing.

Baldwin, M.W., ed. 2005. *Interpersonal Cognition.* New York: Guilford.

Bandura, A. 1998. Mechanisms of Moral Disengagement. In *Origins of Terrorism: Psychologies, Ideologies, Theologies, States of Mind.* Ed. W. Reich. Washington, D.C. Woodrow Wilson Center Press, 161–191.

Bandura, A. 1999. Moral Disengagement in the Perpetration of Inhumanities. *Personality and Social Psychology Review* 3(3): 193–209.

Bandura, A. 2004. The Role of Selective Moral Disengagement in Terrorism and Counterterrorism. In *Understanding Terrorism: Psychosocial Roots, Consequences, and Interventions.* Eds. F. M. Moghaddam and A. J. Marsella. Washington, D.C. American Psychological Association, 121–150.

Bandura, A, C. Barbaranelli, G. V. Caprara, and C.a Pastorelli. 1996. Mechanisms of Moral Disengagement in the Exercise of Moral Agency. *Journal of Personality and Social Psychology* 71(2): 364–374.

Bargh, J. A. 1989. Conditional Automaticity: Varieties of Automatic Influence in Social Perception and Cognition. In *Unintended Thought.* Eds. J. S. Uleman and J. M. Bargh. New York: Guilford, 3–51.

Bargh, J. A. 1990. Auto-Motives: Preconscious Determinants of Social Interaction. In *Handbook of Motivation and Cognition: Foundations of Social Behavior.* Eds. E. T. Higgins and R. M. Sorrentino. New York: Guilford, 93–130.

Bargh, J. A., and K. Barndollar. 1996. Automaticity in Action: The Unconscious as Repository of Chronic Goals and Motives. In *The Psychology of Action: Linking Cognition and Motivation to Behavior*. Eds. P. M. Gollwitzer and J. A. Bargh. New York: Guilford, 457–481.

Bargh, J. A. and M. Ferguson. 2000. Beyond Behaviorism: On the Automaticity of Higher Mental Processes. *Psychological Bulletin* 126: 925–945.

Bargh, J. A. and P. M. Gollwitzer. 1994. Environmental Control of Goal-Directed Action: Automatic and Strategic Contingencies Between Situation and Behavior. In *Integrative Views of Motivation, Cognition, and Emotion*. Ed. W. D. Spaulding. Lincoln: University of Nebraska Press, 71–124.

Bargh, J. A., P. M. Gollwitzer, A. Lee-Chair and K. Barndollar, and R. Trotschel. 2001. The Automated Will: Nonconscious Activation and Pursuit of Behavioral Goals. *Journal of Personality and Social Psychology* 81: 1014–1027.

Barnes, M. L., and R. J. Sternberg. 1989. Social Intelligence and Decoding of Nonverbal Cues. *Intelligence* 13: 263–287.

Baron, R. 1997. The Sweet Smell of … Helping: Effects of Pleasant Ambient Fragrance on Prosocial Behavior in Shopping Malls. *Personality and Social Psychology Bulletin* 23: 498–503.

Baron-Cohen, S., H. A. Ring, S. Wheelwright, E. T. Bullmore, M. J. Brammer, A. Simmons, and S. C. R. Williams. 1999. Social Intelligence in the Normal and Autistic Brain: An fMRI Study. *European Journal of Neuroscience* 11: 1891–1898.

Batson, C. D., P. J. Cochran, M. F. Biederman, J. L. Blosser, M. J. Ryan, and B. Vogt. 1978. Failure to Help When in a Hurry: Callousness or Conflict? *Personality and Social Psychology Bulletin* 4(1): 97–101.

Berg, B. 1978. Helping Behavior on the Gridiron: It Helps if You're Winning. *Psychological Reports* 42: 531–534.

Besser-Jones, L. 2008. Social Psychology, Moral Character, and Moral Fallibility. *Philosophy and Phenomenological Research* LXXVI(2): 310–332.

Blass, T. 1991. Understanding Behavior in the Milgram Obedience Experiment: The Role of Personality, Situations, and Their Interactions. *Journal of Personality and Social Psychology* 60: 398–413.

Blass, T., ed. 2000. *Obedience to Authority: Current Perspectives on the Milgram Paradigm.* Mahwah, NJ: Erlbaum.

Blair, I. V., and M. R. Banaji. 1996. Automatic and Controlling Processes in Stereotype Priming. *Journal of Personality and Social Psychology* 70: 1142–1163.

Blevins, G. and T. Murphy. 1974. Feeling Good and Helping: Further Phone Booth Findings. *Psychological Reports* 34: 326.

Borkenau, P., R. Riemann, F. M. Spinath, and A. Angleitner. 2006. Genetic and Environmental Influences on Person x Situation Profiles. *Journal of Personality* 74(5): 1451–1479.

Bower, G. H. 2007. The Trait versus Situation Debate: A Minimalist View. In *Persons in Context: Building a Science of the Individual.* Eds. Y. Shoda, D. Cervone, and G. Downey. New York: Guilford, 19–42.

Brown, L. T., and R. G. Anthony. 1990. Continuing the Search for Social Intelligence. *Personality and Individual Differences* 11: 463–470.

Bruner, J. S., D. Shapiro, and R. Tagiuri. 1958. The Meaning of Traits in Isolation and in Combination. In *Person Perception and Interpersonal Behavior.* Eds. R. Taguiri and L. Petrollo. Stanford, CA: Stanford University Press, 277–288.

Burley, P. M., and J. McGuinness. 1977. Effects of Social Intelligence on the Milgram Paradigm. *Psychological Reports* 40: 767–770.

Byrne, R. W. 1995. *The Thinking Ape: Evolutionary Origins of Intelligence.* Oxford: Oxford University Press.

Byrne, R. W., and A. Whiten, eds. 1988. *Machiavellian Intelligence: Social Expertise and the Evolution of Intellect in Monkeys, Apes and Humans.* Oxford, UK: Clarendon Press.

Campbell, J. 1999. Can Philosophical Accounts of Altruism Accommodate Experimental Data on Helping Behaviour? *Australasian Journal of Philosophy* 77: 26–45.

Cantor, N. 1978. *Prototypicality and Personality Judgments*. Unpublished doctoral dissertation, Stanford University, Palo Alto, Caifornia.

Cantor, N., and R. Harlowe. 1994. Social Intelligence and Personality: Flexibility Life-Task Pursuit. In *Personality and Intelligence*. Eds. R. J. Sternberg and P. Ruzgis. New York: Cambridge University Press, 137–168.

Cantor, N., and J. F. Kihlstrom. 1987. *Personality and Social Intelligence*. Englewood Cliffs, NJ: Prentice Hall.

Carlson, M., V. Charlin, and N. Miller. 1988. Positive Mood and Helping Behavior: A Test of Six Hypotheses. *Journal of Personality and Social Psychology* 55: 211–229.

Cervone, D., and W. Mischel, eds. 2002. *Advances in Personality Science*. New York: Guilford.

Cervone, D., and Y. Shoda, eds. 1999. *The Coherence of Personality: Social-Cognitive Bases of Consistency, Variability, and Organization*. New York: Guilford.

Chartrand, T. L., and J. A. Bargh. 1996. Automatic Activation of Impression Formation and Memorization Goals: Nonconscious Goal Priming Reproduces Effects of Explicit Task Instructions. *Journal of Personality and Social Psychology 71*: 464–478.

Chodron, P. 2005. *When Things Fall Apart: Heart Advice for Difficult Times*. Boston: Shambhala.

Cunningham, M. 1979. Weather, Mood, and Helping Behavior: The Sunshine Samaritan. *Journal of Personality and Social Psychology* 37: 1947–1956.

Dancy, J. 1993. *Moral Reasons*. Oxford, UK: Blackwell.

Darley, J. M., and D. Batson. 1973. 'From Jerusalem to Jericho': A Study of Situational and Dispositional Variables in Helping Behavior. *Journal of Personality and Social Psychology* 27(1): 100–108.

Devine, P. G. 1989. Stereotypes and Prejudice: Their Automatic and Controlled Components. *Journal of Personality and Social Psychology* 56: 5–18.

Devine, P. G., and M. J. Montieth. 1999. Automaticity and Control in Stereotyping. In *Dual-process Theories in Social Psychology*. Eds. S. Chaiken and Y. Trope. New York: Guilford, 339–360.

Devine, P., E. A. Plant, and B. M. Buswell. 2000. Breaking the Prejudice Habit: Progress and Obstacles. In *Reducing Prejudice and Discrimination*. Ed. S. Oskamp. Mahwah, NJ: Erlbaum, 185–210.

Donnerstein, E, M. Donnerstein, and G. Munger. 1981. Helping Behavior as a Function of Pictorially Induced Moods. *Journal of Social Psychology 97*: 221–225.

Doris, J. M. 1998. Persons, Situations, and Virtue Ethics. *Nous* 32(4): 504–530.

Doris, J. M. 2002. *Lack of Character: Personality and Moral Behavior*. Cambridge, UK: Cambridge University Press.

Doris, J. M. 2005. Précis of Lack of Character. *Philosophy and Phenomenological Research LXXI*(3): 632–634.

Driver, J. 2001. *Uneasy Virtue*. Cambridge, UK: Cambridge University Press.

Ellenberger, H. F. 1970. *The Discovery of the Unconscious: The History and Evolution of Dynamic Psychiatry*. New York: Basic Books.

Elms, A. C. 1972. *Social Psychology and Social Relevance*. Boston: Little, Brown.

Elms, A. C., and S. Milgram. 1966. Personality Characteristics Associated with Obedience and Defiance Toward Authoritative Command. *Journal of Experimental Research in Personality* 1: 282–289.

Fazio, R. H., J. R. Jackson, B. C. Dunton, and C. J. Williams. 1995. Variability in Automatic Activation as an Unobtrusive Measure of Racial Attitudes: A Bona Fide Pipeline? *Journal of Personality and Social Psychology* 69: 1013–1027.

Fishbach, A., R. S. Friedman, and A. W. Kruglanski. 2003. Leading Us Not Into Temptation: Momentary Allurements Elicit Overriding Goal Activation. *Journal of Personality and Social Psychology* 84: 296–309.

Fitzsimons, G. M., and J. A. Bargh. 2003. Thinking of You: Nonconscious Pursuit of Interpersonal Goals Associated with Relationship Partners. *Journal of Personality and Social Psychology* 84: 148–164.

Fitzsimons, G. M., J. Shah, T. L. Chartrand, and J. A. Bargh. 2005. Goals and Labors, Friends and Neighbors: Self-Regulation and Interpersonal Relationships. In *Interpersonal Cognition*. Ed. M. Baldwin. New York: Guilford, 103–125.

Flanagan, O. 1991. *Varieties of Moral Personality: Ethics and Psychological Realism*. Cambridge, MA: Harvard University Press.

Foot, P. 1978. *Virtues and Vices and Other Essays in Moral Philosophy*. Berkeley, CA: University of California Press.

Foot, P. 2001. *Natural Goodness*. Oxford, UK: Clarendon Press.

Ford, M. E., and I. Miura. 1983. *Children's and Adults' Conceptions of Social Competence*. Paper presented at the annual meeting of the American Psychological Association, Anaheim, California.

Ford, M. E., and Tisak, M. S. 1983. A Further Search for Social Intelligence. *Journal of Educational Psychology* 75: 196–206.

Fredrickson N., S. Carlson, and C. W. Ward. 1984. The Place of Social Intelligence in a Taxonomy of Cognitive Abilities. *Intelligence* 8: 315–337.

Funder, D. C. 2001. Personality. *Annual Review of Psychology* 52: 197–221.

Funder, D. C. 2006. Towards a Resolution of the Personality Triad: Persons, Situations, and Behaviors. *Journal of Research in Personality* 40 (1): 21–34.

Gifford, R. 1988. Light, Décor, Arousal, Comfort, and Communication. *Journal of Environmental Psychology* 8: 177–189.

Gilbert, D. T., and J. G. Hixon. 1991. The Trouble with Thinking: Activation and Application of Stereotype Beliefs. *Journal of Personality and Social Psychology* 60: 509–517.

Goldie, P. 2004. *On Personality*. London: Routledge.

Goleman, D. 2006. *Social Intelligence: The New Science of Human Relationships*. New York: Bantam Books.

Gray, J. A., and N. McNaughton. 2000. *The Neuropsychology of Anxiety: An Enquiry into the Functions of the Septo-Hippocampal System*, 2d ed. New York: Oxford University Press.

Greenspan, S., and Love, P. F. 1997. Social Intelligence and Development Disorder: Mental Retardation, Learning Disabilities, and Autism. In *Ellis' Handbook of Mental Deficiency: Psychological Theory and Research*, 3rd ed. Ed. W. E. MacLean. Mahwah, NJ: Erlbaum, 311–342.

Haas, K. 1966. Obedience: Submission to Destructive Orders as Related to Hostility. *Psychological Reports* 19: 32–34.

Haddon, M. 2003. *The Curious Incident of the Dog in the Night-Time*. New York: Random House.

Haney, C., W. Banks, and P. Zimbardo. 1973. Interpersonal Dynamics of a Simulated Prison. *International Journal of Criminology and Penology* 1: 69–97.

Haney, C. and P. Zimbardo. 1977. The Socialization into Criminality: On Becoming a Prisoner and a Guard. In *Law, Justice, and the Individual in Society: Psychological and Legal Issues*. Eds. J. Tapp and F. Levine. New York: Holt, Rinehart, and Winston, 198–223.

Haney, C., and P. Zimbardo. 1998. The Past and Future of U.S. Prison Policy: Twenty-Five Years after the Stanford Prison Experiment. *American Psychologist* 53: 709–727.

Harman, G. 1999. Moral Philosophy Meets Social Psychology: Virtue Ethics and the Fundamental Attribution Error. *Proceedings of the Aristotelian Society* 99: 315–331.

Harman, G. 2000. The Nonexistence of Character Traits. *Proceedings of the Aristotelian Society* 100: 223–226.

Harman, G. 2003. No Character or Personality. *Business Ethics Quarterly* 13: 87–94.

Hartshorne, H., and M. A. May. 1928. *Studies in the Nature of Character*. Vol. I: *Studies in Deceit*. New York: Macmillan.

His Holiness the Dalai Lama. 1999. *Ethics for the New Millennium*. New York: Riverhead Books.

Holekamp, K. E. 2007. Questioning the Social Intelligence Hypothesis. *Trends in Cognitive Science* 11 (2): 65–69.

Hunt, T. 1928. The Measurement of Social Intelligence. *Journal of Applied Psychology* 12: 317–334.

Hursthouse, R. 2007. *Virtue Ethics*. http://plato.stanford.edu/entries/ethics-virtue/ accessed June 13, 2007.

Hursthouse, R. 1999. *On Virtue Ethics*. Oxford, UK: Oxford University Press.

Isen, A. M., and P. F. Levin. 1972. Effect of Feeling Good on Helping: Cookies and Kindness. *Journal of Personality and Social Psychology* 21(3): 384–388.

John, O. P., and S. Srivastava. 1999. The Big Five Trait Taxonomy: History, Measurement, and Theoretical Perspectives. In *Handbook of Personality: Theory and Research* 2d ed. Eds. L. A. Pervin and O. P. John. New York: Guilford, 102–138.

Johnson, R. N. 2003. Virtue and Right. *Ethics* 113: 810–834.

Jones, K., and J. D. Day. 1996. Cognitive Similarities Between Academically and Socially Gifted Students. *Roeper Review* 18(4): 270–274.

Jones, K., and J. D. Day. 1997. Discrimination of Two Aspects of Cognitive-Social Intelligence from Academic Intelligence. *Journal of Educational Psychology* 89(3): 486–497.

Kamtekar, R. 2004. Situationism and Virtue Ethics on the Content of Our Character. *Ethics* 114: 458–491.

Kant, I. 1996. *Practical Philosophy*. Trans. and ed. M. J. Gregor. New York: Cambridge University Press.

Kenrick, D. T., and D. C. Funder. 1988. Profiting from Controversy: Lessons from the Person-Situation Debate. *American Psychologist* 43(1): 23–34.

Kihlstrom, J. F., and N. Cantor. 2000. Social Intelligence. In *Handbook of Intelligence*. Ed. R. J. Sternberg. New York: Cambridge University Press, 359–379.

Kozmitzki, C., and John, O. P. 1993. The Implicit Use of Explicit Conceptions of Social Intelligence. *Personality and Individual Differences* 15: 11–23.

Krahé, B. 1990. *Situation, Cognition and Coherence in Personality: An Individual-Centered Approach*. New York: Cambridge University Press.

Kupperman, J. J. 1991. *Character*. New York: Oxford University Press.

Kupperman, J. J. 2001. The Indispensability of Character. *Philosophy* 76: 239–250.

Kupperman, J. J. 2005. Morality, Ethics, and Wisdom. In *A Handbook of Wisdom: Psychological Perspective*. Eds. R. J. Sternberg and J. Jordan. New York: Cambridge University Press, 245–271.

Kupperman, J. J. 2006. *Six Myths about the Good Life: Thinking about What Has Value*. Indianapolis, Indiana: Hackett.

Latané, B., and J. M. Darley. 1970. *The Unresponsive Bystander: Why Doesn't He Help?* Englewood Cliffs, NJ: Prentice-Hall.

Latané, B., and S. Nida. 1981. Ten Years of Research on Group Size and Helping. *Psychological Bulletin* 89(2): 308–324.

Lee, J-E., J. D. Day, N. M. Meara, and S. Maxwell. 2002. Discrimination of Social Knowledge and Its Flexible Application from Creativity: A Multitrait-Multimethod Approach. *Personality and Individual Differences* 32: 913–928.

Lee, J., C-M. T. Wong, J. D. Day, S. E. Maxwell, and P. Thorpe. 2000. Social and Academic Intelligences: A Multitrait-Multimethod Study of Their Crystallized and Fluid Characteristics. *Personality and Individual Differences* 29: 539–553.

Legree, P.J. 1995. Evidence for an Oblique Social Intelligence Factor Established with a Likert-Based Testing Procedure. *Intelligence* 21: 247–266.

Lepore, L., and R. Brown. 1997. Category and Stereotype Activation: Is Prejudice Inevitable? *Journal of Personality and Social Psychology* 72: 275–287.

Levin, P., and A. Isen. 1975. Further Studies on the Effect of Feeling Good on Helping. *Sociometry* 38: 141–147.

Lord, C. G. 1982. Predicting Behavioral Consistency from an Individual's Perception of Situational Similarities. *Journal of Personality and Social Psychology* 42(6): 1076–1088.

Lowman, R. L., and G. E. Leeman. 1988. The Dimensionality of Social Intelligence: Social Abilities, Interests, and Needs. *Journal of Psychology* 122: 279–290.

Macrae, C. N., G. V. Bodenhausen, and A.B. Milne. 1998. Saying No to Unwanted Thoughts: Self-Focus and the Regulation of Mental Life. *Journal of Personality and Social Psychology* 74(3): 578–589.

Marlowe, H. A. 1986. Social Intelligence: Evidence for Multidimensionality and Construct independence. *Journal of Educational Psychology* 78: 52–58.

Marlowe, H. A., and Bedell, J. R. 1982. Social intelligence: Evidence for Independence of the Construct. *Psychological Reports* 51: 461–462.

Mathews, K., and L. Cannon. 1975. Environmental Noise Level as a Determinant of Helping Behavior. *Journal of Personality and Social Psychology* 32: 571–577.

McCrae, R. R., and P. T. Costa, Jr. 1996. Toward a New Generation of Personality Theories: Theoretical Contexts for the Five-Factor Model. In J. S. Wiggins, 51–87. New York: Guilford.

McDowell, J. 1979. Virtue and Reason. *Monist* 62: 331–350.

McDowell, J. 1995. Two Sorts of Naturalism. In *Virtues and Reasons: Philippa Foot and Moral Theory.* Eds. R. Hursthouse, G. Lawrence, and W. Quinn. Oxford, UK: Clarendon Press, 149–179.

Mendoza-Denton, R., S. H. Park, and A. O'Connor. 2007. Toward a Science of the Social Perceiver. In *Persons in Context: Building a Science of the Individual.* Eds. Y..Shoda, D. Cervone, and G. Downey. New York: Guilford, 211–225.

Merritt, Ma. 2000. Virtue Ethics and Situationist Personality Psychology. *Ethical Theory and Moral Practice* 3: 365–383.

Milgram, S. 1974. *Obedience to Authority: An Experimental View.* New York: HarperCollins.

Milgram, S. 1977. *The Individual in a Social World: Essays and Experiments.* Reading, MA: Addison-Wesley.

Miller, C. 2003. Social Psychology and Virtue Ethics. *The Journal of Ethics* 7: 365–392.

Miller, C. Social Psychology, Mood, and Helping: Mixed Results for Virtue Ethics. Under review. *The Journal of Ethics.* Special Issue on Situationism (forthcoming).

Mischel, W. 1968. *Personality and Assessment.* New York: Wiley.

Mischel, W. 1973. Toward a Cognitive Social Learning Reconceptualization of Personality. *Psychological Review* 80(4): 252–283.

Mischel, W. 1999. Personality Coherence and Dispositions in a Cognitive-Affective Personality System (CAPS) Approach. In *The Coherence of Personality: Social-Cognitive Bases of Consistency, Variability, and Organization.* Eds. D. Cervone and Y. Shoda. New York: Guilford, 37–60.

Mischel, W. 2007. Toward a Science of the Individual: Past, Present, and Future? In *Persons in Context: Building a Science of the Individual.* Eds. Y. Shoda, D. Cervone, and G. Downey. New York: Guilford, 263–277.

Mischel, W., and Y. Shoda. 1995. A Cognitive-Affective System Theory of Personality: Reconceptualizing Situations, Dispositions, Dynamics, and Invariance in Personality Structure. *Psychological Review* 102(2): 246–268.

Mischel, W., and Y. Shoda. 1999. Integrating Dispositions and Processing Dynamics within a Unified Theory of Personality: The Cognitive-Affective Personality System. In *Handbook of Personality: Theory and Research* 2d ed. Eds. L. A. Pervin and O. P. John. New York: Guilford, 197–218.

Mischel, W., Y. Shoda, and O. Ayduk. 2008. *Introduction to Personality: Toward an Integrative Science of the Person,* 8th ed. Hoboken, NJ: Wiley.

Monteith, M. J. 1993. Self-Regulation of Prejudiced Responses: Implications for Progress in Prejudice Reduction Efforts. *Journal of Personality and Social Psychology* 65: 469–485.

Montmarquet, J. 2003. Moral Character and Social Science Research. *Philosophy* 78: 355–368.

Moss, F. A., and T. Hunt. 1927. Are You Socially Intelligent? *Scientific American* 137: 108–110.

Newcomb, T. M. 1929. *The Consistency of Certain Extrovert-Introvert Behavior Patterns in 51*

Problem Boys. New York: Columbia University, Teachers College, Bureau of Publications.
Pettit, P. 2001. *A Theory of Freedom: From the Psychology to the Politics of Agency*. Oxford, UK: Polity Press.
Pollard, B. 2003. Can Virtuous Actions Be Both Habitual and Rational? *Ethical Theory and Moral Practice* 6: 411–425.
Rosenhan, D. L., P. Salovey, and K. Harris. 1981. The Joys of Helping: Focus on Attention Mediates the Impact of Positive Affect on Altruism. *Journal of Personality and Social Psychology* 40: 800–905.
Riggio, R. E., J. Messamer, and B. Throckmorton. 1991. Social and Academic Intelligence: Conceptually Distinct but Overlapping Constructs. *Personality and Individual Differences* 12(7): 695–702.
Ross, L., and R. E. Nisbett. 1991. *The Person and the Situation: Perspectives of Social Psychology*. New York: McGraw-Hill.
Sabini, J., and M. Silver. 2005. Lack of Character? Situationism Critiqued. *Ethics* 115: 535–562.
Schaller, M., and R. Cialdini. 1990. Happiness, Sadness, and Helping: A Motivational Integration. In *Handbook of Motivation and Cognition*. Eds. E. Higgins and R. Sorrentino. New York: Guilford, 265–296.
Schneider, R. J., O. L. Ackerman, and R. Kanfer. 1996. To 'Act Wisely in Human Relations': Exploring the Dimensions of Social Competence. *Personality and Individual Differences* 21: 469–482.
Shah, J. 2003. Automatic for the People: How Representations of Significant Others Implicitly Affect Goal Pursuit. *Journal of Personality and Social Psychology* 84: 661–681.
Sherman, N. 2005. *Stoic Warriors: The Ancient Philosophy Behind the Military Mind*. New York: Oxford University Press.
Shoda, Y., and S. J. LeeTiernan. 2002. What Remains Invariant? Finding Order within a Person's Thoughts, Feelings, and Behaviors across Situations. In *Advances in Personality Science*. Eds. Daniel Cervone and Walter Mischel. New York: Guilford, 241–270.
Shoda, Y., and W. Mischel. 1993. Cognitive Social Approach to Dispositional Inferences: What if the Perceiver is a Cognitive Social Theorist? *Personality and Social Psychology Bulletin* 19(5): 574–585.
Shoda, Y., and W. Mischel. 1996. Toward a Unified, Intra-Individual Dynamic Conception of Personality. *Journal of Research in Personality* 30: 414–428.
Shoda, Y., and W. Mischel. 1998. Reconciling Processing Dynamics and Personality Dispositions. *Annual Review of Psychology* 49: 229–258.
Shoda, Y., W. Mischel, and J. C. Wright. 1989. Intuitive Interactionism in Person Perception: Effects of Situation-Behavior Relations on Dispositional Judgments. *The Journal of Personality and Social Psychology* 56(1): 441–453.
Shoda, Y., W. Mischel, and J.C. Wright. 1993. The Role of Situational Demands and Cognitive Competencies in Behavior Organization and Personality Coherence. *Journal of Personality and Social Psychology* 65(5): 1023–1035.
Shoda, Y., W. Mischel, and J. C. Wright. 1994. Intraindividual Stability in the Organization and Patterning of Behavior: Incorporating Psychological Situations in the Idiographic Analysis of Personality. *Journal of Personality and Social Psychology* 67(4): 674–687.
Sinclair, L., and Z. Kunda. 1997. *Feedback-Dependent Evaluation of Evaluators: Motivated Application and Inhibition of Stereotypes*. University of Waterloo. Unpublished manuscript.
Slote, M. 2001. *Morals From Motives*. Oxford, UK: Oxford University Press.
Smith, M. 1994. *The Moral Problem*. Oxford, UK: Blackwell.
Snow, N. E. 2008. Virtue and Flourishing. *Journal of Social Philosophy* XXXIX(2): 225–245.
Sreenivasan, G. 2002. Errors about Errors: Virtue Theory and Trait Attribution. *Mind* 111: 47–68.
Sterelny, K. 1998. Intentional Agency and Metarepresentation Hypothesis. *Mind and Language* 13(1): 11–28.

Sternberg, R. J. 1998. A Balance Theory of Wisdom. *Review of General Psychology* 2: 47–365.
Sternberg, R. J. and C. Smith. 1985 . Social Intelligence and Decoding Skill in Nonverbal Communication. *Social Cognition* 3 (2): 168–192.
Sternberg, R. J., B. E. Conway, J. L. Keatron, and M. Bernstein. 1981. People's Conceptions of Intelligence. *Journal of Personality and Social Psychology* 41: 37–55.
Strang, R. 1930. Measures of Social Intelligence. *Psychotherapy* 27: 263–269.
Stricker, L. J., and D. A. Rock. 1990. Interpersonal Competence, Social Intelligence, and General Ability. *Personality and Individual Differences* 11: 833–839.
Swanton, C. 2003. *Virtue Ethics: A Pluralistic View*. Oxford,UK: Oxford University Press.
Taylor, E. H. 1990. The Assessment of Social Intelligence. *Psychotherapy* 27: 445–457.
Thomson, J. J. 1996. Evaluatives and Directives. In Gilbert Harman and Judith Jarvis Thompson. *Moral Relativism and Moral Objectivity*. Cambridge, MA: Blackwell.
Thomson, J. J. 1997. The Right and the Good. *The Journal of Philosophy* XCIV(6): 273–298.
Thorndike, E. L. 1920. Intelligence and Its Use. *Harper's Magazine* 140: 227–235.
Vansteelandt, K., and I. Van Mechelen. 1998. Individual Differences in Situation-Behavior Profiles: A Triple Typology Model. *Journal of Personality and Social Psychology* 75(3): 751–765.
Velleman, J. D. 2000. *The Possibility of Practical Reason*. Oxford, UK: Clarendon Press.
Vernon, P. E. 1933. Some Characteristics of the Good Judge of Personality. *Journal of Social Psychology* 4: 42–57.
Webber, J. 2006a. Virtue, Character, and Situation. *Journal of Moral Philosophy* 3(2): 193–213.
Webber, J. 2006b. Character, Consistency, and Classification. *Mind: A Quarterly Review of Philosophy* 115(459): 651–658.
Webber, J. 2007. Character, Common-Sense, and Expertise. *Ethical Theory and Moral Practice* 10(1): 89–104.
Wechsler, D. 1958. *The Measurement and Appraisal of Adult Intelligence* 4th ed. Baltimore: Williams and Wilkins.
Wedeck, J. 1947. The Relationship Between Personality and Psychological Ability. *British Journal of Psychology* 36: 133–151.
Weis, S. and H. Suss. 2007. Reviving the Search for Social Intelligence—A Multitrait-Multimethod Study of Its Structure and Construct Validity. *Personality and Individual Differences* 42: 3–14.
Weyant, J., and R. Clark. 1977. Dimes and Helping: The Other Side of the Coin. *Personality and Social Psychology Bulletin* 3: 107–110.
Whiten, A., and Byrne, R., eds. 1997. *Machiavellian Intelligence II: Extensions and Evaluations*. Cambridge, UK: Cambridge University Press.
Wielenberg, E. J. 2006. Saving Character. *Ethical Theory and Moral Practice* 9: 461–491.
Wiggins, J. S. ed. 1996. The Five-Factor Model of Personality: Theoretical Perspectives. New York: Guilford.
Wong, C., J. D. Day, S. E. Maxwell, and N. M. Meara. 1995. A Multitrait-Multimethod Study of Academic and Social Intelligence in College Students. *Journal of Educational Psychology* 87(1): 117–133.
Wright, .C., and W. Mischel. 1988. Conditional Hedges and the Intuitive Psychology of Traits. *Journal of Personality and Social Psychology* 55(3): 454–469.
Wright, J. C., and W. Mischel. 1987. A Conditional Approach to Dispositional Constructs: The Local Predictability of Social Behavior. *Journal of Personality and Social Psychology* 53(6): 1159–1177.
Zagzebski, L. T. 1996. *Virtues of the Mind: An Inquiry into the Nature of Virtue and the Ethical Foundations of Knowledge*. New York: Cambridge University Press.
Zimbardo, P. 2007. *The Lucifer Effect: Understanding How Good People Turn Evil*. New York: Random House.
Zimbardo, P. G., C. Maslach, and C. Haney. 2000. Reflections on the Stanford Prison Experiment: Genesis, Transformations, Consequences. In *Obedience to Authority: Current Perspectives on the Milgram Paradigm*. Ed. T Blass. Mahwah, NJ: Erlbaum.

INDEX

18841070R00082

Made in the USA
San Bernardino, CA
21 December 2018